Praise for An Insider's Guide

"I've been in federal government contracting for 20+ years, selling my last company in late 2017. I rarely regret anything in life, but I regret that I did not have this book when I was running my companies... I could have easily doubled the annual revenue. The lessons in this book are informative and tactical, with clear recommendations for how a GovCon small business could succeed at various stages. *This is hands down the best book for anyone in Government Contracting.* I own many books, but this is the one I've wished was available. It is now."

Neil McDonnell
GovCon Chamber of Commerce

"As a former federal contracting officer, PTAC counselor, coach, and trainer, I've taken in a ton of training and have read many books over the years. *An Insider's Guide to Winning Government Contracts is one of the most practical books I've ever read on the subject of winning government contracts.* This book will not only help you win but break through the barriers that have been holding you back. It will take you to a whole new level. This is definitely a book where you will receive a return on your investment many times over."

Carroll Bernard, Govology

"*The return on my investment in this book was immediate!* This book is a striking reminder that business development in the federal sector is heavily nuanced. There is a mental conditioning aspect to this book that is rare among business development books. Josh frames the ever-changing federal business opportunity landscape in a way that is easily understood and thought provoking."

Chris Smith
Anderson & Catania Surety Services

"I've read many books from other well-known professionals and speakers and this one takes you to the next level. The book was transformative because of its unique insight into the procurement process. *One of the best resources I've ever read.* Different from all the other books I've ever read on government sales because you can now apply what you've learned."

Paul Myer, Amazon Review

"Government contracting advice that works! Mr. Frank's no-nonsense approach to identifying government contract opportunities in the pre-acquisition phase is extremely helpful. The information is easy to follow and it works! *This book is a must read if you are wanting to expand and grow your business in the government sector.*"

Stephanie Masters
Crowned Grace International

"I have so many items highlighted and pages dog-eared from all of valuable information I have gleaned from this book. If you are new to the federal market or even an experienced pro, *I know there is something that will help you win business from this book.* I am excited to put these practices in place and grow our federal business!

Juliann Poff, Gannett Fleming

"For some time, I along with several of my colleagues have searched in vain for a book on government sales that focuses on the business aspect, not simply your NAICS codes, creating a capability statement, or all the other standard recommendations that you see in all the other books on Amazon. After purchasing several books by other well-known government "experts," I can finally say that we found the right book! I found myself laughing and enjoying the process of learning these techniques from page to page. *Just like the author, this book is an invaluable asset that I will continue to look to for leading guidance.*"

Danielle Jackson, Digital Interface

"Outstanding guidance for new or experienced business development professionals. I'm not new to business, but I'm new to business development with the federal government. This book did a great job answering the question "how do I tackle this new role?" The overall strategy, flow of the discussion, and concrete recommendations on "how" to do it have been extremely helpful. If you are new to BD or are just needing to form a solid BD plan, I strongly recommend this book."

James Lutz, SANS Institute

"Excellent read. I'd buy it again! *This book has been a game changer.* Government Contracting is all about the long game and Joshua Frank provides an insightful perspective of how to best develop a winning strategy."

Reggie Polk, Polk & Associates

"I have been working in the government space for the last 15 years, but always feel that I can learn more. *This book has changed some of my strategies for winning government contracts!* If you want to easily apply what you've learned, then this is the book for you. I literally took two processes from this book and immediately began implementing them in my strategy. I'm sure I will implement more."

Alexis Earnest, T4S Partners

"I first heard Josh speak at a Government Conference 4 years ago. His presentation was right on point for what I needed to know - my personal next steps. I've learned so much applying his strategies as our company has grown. *This book is so intense and applicable TODAY that I'm buying each person in the company a copy.* Josh is definitely "The Professor of Government Sales." Thank you! We wouldn't be where we are without you."

Lisa Lowery, Adapt Construction

"Joshua provides information that is unique, relevant, practical, and entertaining."

Jason Whetsell
Gabriel Enterprises Consulting Group

An Insider's Guide to Winning Government Contracts

Real-World Strategies, Lessons and Recommendations

Second Edition

Joshua P. Frank

Requests to the Publisher for permission should be addressed to RSM Federal, 13 Amber Wave Ct. OFallon, MO 63366 or mail@rsmfederal.com. Liability / Disclaimer: Although the author has used his best efforts in preparing this book, he makes no representations or warranties with respect to the accuracy or completeness of the contents of this book.

No warranty may be created or extended by sales representatives, strategic partners, affiliates, or written sales collateral. The lessons, recommendations, and strategies contained in this book may not be applicable to your specific business requirements. You should consult with a professional consultant where appropriate. The author shall not be liable for any loss of revenue or profit or incidental damages. For more information about RSM Federal, visit www.rsmfederal.com. For more information about the author, visit www.authorjoshfrank.com.

Second Edition
ISBN 978-1-7336009-2-7 (pbk)
ISBN 978-1-7336009-3-4 (ebk)

First edition published 2019
ISBN 978-1-7336009-0-3 (pbk); ISBN 978-1-7336009-1-0 (ebk)

www.authorjoshfrank.com and www.rsmfederal.com

Printed in the United States of America
1 2 3 4 5 6 7 8 9 10

This book is dedicated to my wife Lisa, daughter Jordan, and son Michael. My family is my world.

Contents

Foreword
Carroll Bernard, Co-Founder of Govology.com

W hether you are new to government sales or you've been selling for years, "An Insider's Guide To Winning Government Contracts" will *make you think differently about how you sell*.

If you happen to be new to the government marketplace, then it's a good day to be you! You have an opportunity to learn and implement strategies and tactics that take many of today's top contractors years to understand. The unfortunate reality is that many small businesses enter the realm of federal contracting and become frustrated and confused.

By the time you finish reading this book, you will have powerful concepts and strategies at your fingertips. If you *apply* these strategies, not only will you win government contracts, you will do so in a shorter period of time. You will gain massive advantages in head-to-head competitions and you will improve your win-ratio.

The author, Joshua Frank, is known as a "thought-leader" in the government market. He combines an expertise in government sales with the thought-leadership of a business professional that knows his craft.

It is no surprise that over the years Joshua has come to be known as "The Professor of Government Sales." He has spent years learning, crafting, studying, and practicing what it takes to win. And now you have access to some of his strategies, packaged nicely in a book, that you can take with you and reference anytime, anywhere.

As a professional speaker, Joshua supports and regularly speaks at many of our nation's largest government conferences and symposiums. Over the last ten years, he has trained more than 10,000 business professionals (both large and small businesses). If you ask Joshua how he measures success, he will tell you there is only one metric - *whether or not his clients win contracts*.

Over the last ten years, the concepts and strategies in this book have helped his clients win more than $2.6 Billion in small business government contracts and more than $30 Billion in multiple award contract vehicles.

In 2016, I attended a conference in St. Louis Missouri hosted by the Association of Procurement Technical Assistance Centers (APTAC). During the event, Joshua Frank presented 'Advanced Teaming Strategies' to a group of approximately 600 PTAC counselors.

Not long after the start of the session, a PTAC Program Manager ran out of the room and made a beeline to my exhibit booth. She said, "Oh wow, Carroll - you have got to get Joshua on Govology!"

I immediately walked over and joined the session. I'm glad I did because it was one of the best small business training events I've ever seen. I know that's a bold statement, but before I started Govology, I was a Contracting Officer for the Department of Veterans Affairs (VA); a Business Opportunities Specialist for the Small Business Administration (SBA), and a PTAC Counselor.

I immediately approached Joshua after his session and the rest is history. I'm proud to announce that Joshua and his team at RSM Federal are now one of Govology's strategic partners. You can find Joshua presenting webinars at Govology.com.

Since 2016, Joshua has been an Adjunct Faculty Instructor for Govology. His thought-leadership, concepts, and strategies are some of the best in the industry. This sentiment is not just my opinion; we frequently hear this feedback from our students and companies around the country.

If you aren't familiar with Govology, we provide online education for government contractors. What makes us different is our passion for collaborating with some of the nation's most recognized and sought-after experts like Joshua Frank.

We collaborate with experts working at private firms, non-profits, universities, and government agencies across the country who also share our mission of supporting small businesses.

Most important, Govology has nationwide partnerships with more than fifty (50) Procurement Technical Assistance Centers (PTACs). The PTAC program is funded in part by the Department of Defense (DoD) to provide *free counseling and guidance* for businesses entering the government market.

Many of our PTAC partners offer their clients free or low-cost access to Govology webinars and on-demand courses. If you've never heard of PTAC, you should become familiar with this great program and leverage their services as you navigate the government marketplace. To learn more about this program and to locate a PTAC in your state, visit www.dla.mil/SmallBusiness/PTAP/.

There are three fundamental truths that I have discovered over a decade of coaching and training thousands of small businesses.

- **Truth #1** - Knowledge only becomes power *through its application*, which is something you will learn from Joshua in this book.

- **Truth #2** - Contractors will likely fail if they try to go it alone. If you want to be a DIY contractor, the odds will not be in your favor.

- **Truth #3** - No "single" expert or organization individually has all of the answers to every question you will ever have when it comes to government contracting. This is why, as you build your foundation for success in the government marketplace, it is essential that you develop and maintain a network of experts to provide guidance when you need it. In Napoleon Hill's book *Think and Grow Rich*, he calls this the "power of the mastermind."

The case studies, lessons, strategies, and recommendations in this book provide real-world examples that will complement, build upon, and enhance the advice and recommendations you receive from your local PTAC counselor and other small business experts.

These chapters are quick-reads. There are so many great concepts and strategies that whether you start at page one or jump to an interesting chapter, you can't go wrong.

Joshua's approach is refreshing and it is no surprise that he is one of the premier small business coaches in the nation.

Enjoy, take notes, and learn from "The Professor of Government Sales."

- Carroll Bernard, Co-Founder and CEO, Govology

Author's Introduction

I have supported the government market for almost 30 years. I have served in the military. I have worked for Fortune 100 and small business. I ran the Department of Defense for MasterCard Worldwide in Washington DC and I have served in multiple program, business development, and executive roles. I have sold billions of dollars in products and services to the armed services and federal agencies.

In 2008, I started RSM Federal, a training, coaching, and management consultant firm that provides businesses with laser-focused and *tailored* step-by-step strategies for winning government contracts.

Winning government contracts is not easy. The strategies required to win a government contract are the same, regardless of the size of your company. Yes, there are additional strategies for taking advantage of socio-economic set-asides, but the marketing, prospecting, sales, teaming, and proposal processes are pretty much the same.

Where the majority of my clients are small business, 20% are companies with more than $250 million in annual revenue.

This book was specifically written for entrepreneurs, small business owners and professionals, as well as small business counselors and advisors.

If you own or work for a large company, the basics for business, sales, and relationships do not change because you have ten or ten-thousand employees.

95% of the concepts, strategies, and recommendations in this book are market and industry agnostic. These strategies are tailored to the government market but the business concepts are just as valuable in the commercial space.

In 2008, I published *The Government Sales Manual* with the eighth edition released in 2018. With more than 460 pages and hundreds of step-by-step strategies, it is one of the more comprehensive small business resources on the market for government sales.

If you are new to the government market, *The Government Sales Manual* is designed to help you win contracts and accelerate your entry into the market. You can learn more about the manual at rsmfederal.com or on Amazon. *(Check both sites since I often run discounts on one or the other.)* Due to hundreds of graphics, tables, and figures, it is only available in print (unless you're a member of the Federal Access Knowledge-Base where you have access to a digital version).

This book, *An Insider's Guide to Winning Government Contracts: Real-World Strategies, Lessons, and Recommendations*, marks the 10th anniversary of my company, RSM Federal. I have trained thousands of companies, other business coaches and consultants, and countless small business counselors. RSM Federal's clients and Federal Access Members have won more than $2.6 billion in government contracts and more than $30 billion in multiple award umbrella contracts.

Teaching and coaching are my passion. So, for the 10th anniversary, I want to share several real-world lessons and strategies that will change how you approach not only government sales, but the market as a whole.

There are thousands of consultants and resources that will tell you *what to do.*

There are hundreds of business books on Amazon that will tell you *what to do.*

There are training events, webinars, and conference seminars that will tell you *what to do.*

This is a by-product of how we learn. In general terms, we teach what we were taught. As a result, many educators in the market teach the same information they were taught, *regardless of whether it makes sense from a business perspective.*

Whether it is a book, a mentor, a consultant, a webinar, or a training session, most of what you are taught is the same generic information.

Because of this, there is a high failure rate for government contractors and this should not be the case! There are hundreds of resources to help minority, woman, veteran, and small businesses. Every one of these resources provide value. They all provide concrete advice and direction. They all help identify *what you need to do*.

I want to help you *apply* what you have learned.

It is not what you know. It is not what you have been taught. *It is how you apply it*. This is what separates companies that win contracts from companies that do not. This simple, yet complex concept is why companies that use these strategies have won billions in government contracts.

It is not magic.

I am not going to preach the same generic information that you will find in most books on "how to sell to the government."

I want to arm you with concepts, strategies, and recommendations that will help you mature and generate more revenue. I am going to apply lessons and case studies to what you have already learned and experienced.

Whether you are new to government sales or you have been selling to the government for years, the topics and strategies in this book are designed to make you *think*.

My objective is to change how you approach government sales.

I also write the way I talk. That is to say I go off on tangents, which I will do throughout the book. None of the activities required to win a government contract are performed in a vacuum. If you are writing a proposal, it is next to impossible to write a winning proposal without having strong back office processes, market intelligence from a strong business development strategy, and understanding the value of your solutions.

As a result, regardless of the topic being discussed, we will take detours now and then. Because of this, I highly recommend you grab a highlighter before you jump into the chapters. You are likely to find concepts and strategies that you will want to implement.

Second and Revised Edition

This is the second edition of *An Insider's Guide to Winning Government Contracts*. When I first published this book in January 2019, I had hoped that I would make the top 100 business books for government. I was pleasantly surprised. It catapulted to number one bestseller the day it released.

Since launching this book, the market response has been surreal. I've sold and distributed more than 10,000 copies via Amazon, book signings, and other events. LinkedIn exploded. I received hundreds of messages saying I changed their outlook on business. Companies have reached out telling me how excited they are and telling me which strategies they implemented and the explosive results.

Nothing rejuvenates me more than being contacted by folks that I've never met - saying how excited they are about what they've learned! In October 2019, I keynoted the Annual Government Symposium for the Governor's office in Utah. After the keynote, a business owner walked up to me and said, "Josh, you don't know me, but I've read your book and wanted you to know that you have changed my life."

That's when I knew I had met the professional and personal standards that I envisioned when I started writing this book.

As for target market, these strategies are not only for small business. It doesn't matter if you're a small or large company. The value in executing the right tactics and strategies are market and industry agnostic. This book may have been written for the small business community, but it has been well received by business professionals in large companies as well.

When the Executive Director for a billion-dollar Defense contractor asks all of her business developers to read this book, it's clear that these tactics and strategies transcend business size.

I measure my personal success not by the number of clients, but by the *success that our clients achieve*. I've had countless companies call, email, and text that they've won millions of dollars. Prior to the launch of this book in early 2019, my company, RSM Federal, had helped companies win $2 billion in government contracts. In just the past year, that number increased to $2.6 billion with hundreds of new companies registering for the Federal Access Knowledge-Base for tactics, strategies, and templates.

This second and revised edition expands and provides updates on government systems. One of the first major changes was the consolidation of the GSA Schedule program. The shift to a consolidated schedule will continue through 2020 and probably 2021.

Another subject matter expert (SME) and author called me and asked how I was going to handle all the changes. She said, *"Josh, you refer throughout the book to FedBizOpps for finding opportunities. That site doesn't exist anymore!"*

I hung up the phone, thought for a moment, and took a heavy sigh. She wasn't kidding. I did a quick search and found FedBizOpps 38 times; FBO eight times; System for Award Management 16 times; SAM 98 times; and FPDS 35 times. That's 195 updates and that's only half of the systems I touch on... and all of these changes took place in less than 10 months.

I spent two months revising this book and *I enjoyed every second of it!* In late 2019, the Integrated Award Environment (IAE) began to take shape. FedBizOpps (FBO) was integrated into the new System for Award Management (SAM) environment. As I write this, I'm currently a beta-tester for the new Federal Procurement Data System (FPDS) which will be integrated into SAM in 2020.

This revised edition provides updates throughout when referring to and discussing these systems. I've added a new chapter on the Integrated Award Environment (IAE) and discuss the current and future direction of these systems. You'll find that except for a few instances, FedBizOpps / FBO is now referred to as SAM.

There is also a new chapter on the importance of category management which now impacts most products and services. This chapter discusses how and why you should take category management into account as part of your overall market and sales strategy.

Finally, I want to thank all the readers and organizations that bought this book and provided their feedback. I hazard to guess that half of all books sold have come from referrals. That's amazing and a validation that I met my objective when I started down this path.

I hope you enjoy this book as much as I enjoyed writing it!
To your success in government sales.
Joshua P. Frank

Chapter 1.
Government Sales Is A Long-Game

Winning government contracts is not simple. If it were simple, everyone would be winning contracts. The good news is that any company can succeed in government sales with an understanding of the market, perseverance, *strong* business strategy, and time.

It takes experience. Yes, there are exceptions. Some companies that sell products can win a contract in a matter of weeks. I have helped product companies get set-up and win a contract in a matter of days. But for *most* products and services, you will rarely find "low-hanging-fruit." And even when you find low-hanging fruit, you will be trying to figure out how you lost to a company whose pricing is lower than what you were given from the manufacturer.

There are companies that will send you an email saying:

"Look! The government buys billions of dollars for your products or services. You are missing out on millions of dollars in contracts! We will help you get a GSA Schedule contract. If you get a GSA Schedule, you will have access to "low-hanging-fruit."

Uh-huh. If it were only that simple.

More than 50% of GSA Schedule holders fail to successfully win contracts. Yes, really. The last time I reviewed contractor data, of the ~20,000 companies with a GSA Schedule, 10,000 failed to meet the $25,000 annual threshold in sales. That is 10,000 companies with a government contract vehicle and almost no sales! Of those companies, 7,000 failed to make a single penny. Not one cent.

However, if you have a GSA Schedule and you understand how to use it, it is an outstanding contract vehicle that can make you a lot of money.

My point is that contract vehicles are nothing more than a press-release if you do not know how to take advantage them.

Now, I want you to imagine the following scenario. It happens in every industry, *every day* across the country. Two companies sell the exact same products or services. They enter the government market at the exact same time. The owners of both companies have the exact same level of education. They bought the exact same books on Amazon. They even hired the same government consultants. They attended the same government conferences last year, attended the same webinars, and attended the same training events. Both companies had the exact same training and resources.

One of these companies won $3.4 million in government contracts and doubled the size of their company. The other company did not win a single contract.

What explains this?

GSA Schedules are the most recognized contract vehicles in government sales.

How can half of all GSA Schedule holders fail to win contracts? How can two companies educate themselves using the exact same training resources and one succeeds and one fails?

The answer is multi-faceted and one of the most important lessons in this book.

First, selling to the government is like being pregnant. You are either serious about selling to the government or you are not. Government sales is not a part-time job. It is not something you dabble-in. At least one person in your company should be focused on government sales.

That being said, I've helped many companies develop a time-management plan that allows their existing employees or the president of the company to spend a couple hours a week positioning for government sales. It can be done but you must be absolutely focused and not wasting time on frivolous activities.

To successfully win multiple contracts, you need a strong business development strategy. You need a strong teaming strategy. You need a strong proposal process. You need strong back-office operations.

You need time. You need experience.

Selling to the government is a long-game.

It takes many companies three to five years to win a government contract. As you can imagine, if it takes that long, most companies give-up long before the three-year mark. Most companies that win government contracts, as either a prime or subcontractor, do so in their first eighteen months.

Eighteen months? Does it really take that long? Yes, selling to the government is a strategic decision for your company. Do it right and you can make millions. This does not mean you can't win contracts in less time. But for larger contracts, it takes time to position, build the right relationships, and collect the necessary market intelligence to be competitive.

One company wins $3.4 million and the other does not make a single penny. This happens every day because there is a difference between educating yourself on selling to the government and understanding how to *apply* what you have learned. This is one of the most important lessons that I cover with my clients.

It is not about what you learn. It is how you apply it.

One of the more common complaints I hear from small business professionals is, "There is entirely too much information! Everyone I talk to says I need to do these three or five or eight things. They are all different! They all seem to make sense but every time I talk to someone else, I get different guidance. I'm receiving conflicting priorities. Seriously! What do I need to do to win contracts?"

You can attend dozens of webinars and training events. You can buy dozens of books on "how to sell to the government," but if you do not learn how to *apply* what you have been taught, you will be running around in circles.

I specialize in providing companies with tailored step-by-step tactics and strategies for successfully engaging the government market. I'm also well known for setting brutally realistic expectations. Our average client will win a new government contract in six to fourteen months.

Selling to the government can be very lucrative but it takes patience and time.

The chapters in this book are case studies and lessons on how to better apply what you have learned. I always recommend that you start with the PTAC and in parallel gaining access to RSM Federal's knowledge-base called Federal Access (FA). You can access every resource, strategy, training video, and template for $59 a month. You can visit https://www.rsmfederal.com/FA for more information. Then when you're ready, you can reach out to a coach to help you accelerate. By the way, that's why companies hire business coaches – to accelerate their market entry.

There are several things you can do right now to accelerate your sales-cycle. First, set realistic expectations. Selling to the government is a long-game. Second, do not simply educate yourself. All those webinars and books are critical to getting smarter. But you need tactics and strategies for applying what you have learned.

You find an opportunity but you know you cannot go after it on your own. You simply do not have the experience or past performance required to be competitive. You are told to go team with other companies. How do you find companies to team with? How do you know if they will be competitive? How do you approach them? What do you say? How do you convince them to bring you onto their team? What documentation should you give them?

You are told to call the small business office for a federal agency. What are you supposed to ask? When they ask for your capability statement, what are you going to tailor on your statement before sending it? When the small business office tells you to go to the Integrated Award Environment (IAE) or the System for Award Management (SAM) (SAM is part of IAE) to find bid opportunities, how are you going to respond? What research will you do before you call the small business office?

You are told to use SAM or a bid-matching tool to find opportunities. That's great but companies that are successful in government sales focus their business development on **pre-acquisition activities**. Requests for proposals (RFP) and requests for quotes (RFQ) are not pre-acquisition. They are acquisition.

So, if you know that companies that win contracts focus their activities in pre-acquisition and RFPs are post-acquisition, how do you resolve this? Where do you focus? How do you get out of the cycle of responding to RFPs and start building pre-acquisition relationships?

You plan to go after an opportunity that has an incumbent. When you ask for help, you are told to research the existing contract. How do you figure out who the incumbent is? Where do you find the contract value for the base year of their contract? What was the total value of the contract with all option years? Which labor categories are being used? How many contracts does the incumbent have in that agency and all other agencies? How to you figure out if you'll be competitive on the recompete? Do they have a GSA Schedule? Generally, what is their pricing for each labor category?

When you look into the market and ask yourself, "How did that company win those contracts?" The answer is time, perseverance, and understanding it is not what you learn but how you apply it.

So, do you need to realign your expectations? Do you have the right tactics and strategies to apply what you have learned?

Something to think about.

Chapter 2.
The Integrated Award Environment (IAE) and Other Updates

This is one of several new chapters I've included in the second edition. Government systems are finally coming into the twenty-first century. The changes to these systems and procurement mechanisms have taken place in just twelve months since this book was first released.

I'm going to briefly discuss the following systems and updates:

- FedBizOpps (FBO) migration to SAM
- FPDS migration to SAM
- DUNS migration to SAMMI
- GSA Schedule Consolidation

The Integrated Award Environment (IAE)

Let's start with the Integrated Award Environment (IAE). The following is from the General Services Administration's (GSA) website:[1] *The Integrated Award Environment (IAE) is a Presidential E-Government initiative managed by GSA. We use innovative processes and technologies to improve systems and operations for those who:*

- *Award;*
- *Administer; or*
- *Receive federal financial assistance via grants, loans, **contracts**, and intergovernmental transactions.*

---

[1] www.gsa.gov/iae

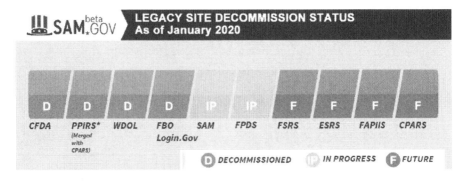

LEGACY SITE DECOMMISSION STATUS
As of January 2020

| D | D | D | D | IP | IP | F | F | F | F |
| CFDA | PPIRS* (Merged with CPARS) | WDOL | FBO | SAM Login.Gov | FPDS | FSRS | ESRS | FAPIIS | CPARS |

D DECOMMISSIONED   **IP** IN PROGRESS   **F** FUTURE

Several additional metrics for the Integrated Award Environment (IAE) : NOTE [2]

- *IAE systems have an average of 1.7 million users; In SAM alone, there's an average of 621,000 active registered entities which includes an average of more than 59,000 new or renewed registrants.*
- *More than $3.98 Trillion in federal awards annually and an average of 4.4 million transactions per month are reported in IAE systems.*
- *The IAE systems generate more than 498 million hits or page views per month, including an average of almost 4.5 million searches per month in SAM alone.*

Already, the Wage and Determinations listings (Service Contract Act / SCA) has migrated from the Department of Labor's website to the new System for Award Management (SAM) website. But the most recent (and frustrating migration) was FedBizOpps. For several decades, government contractors have used FedBizOpps (FBO) as the central gateway to government sales. In late 2019, FBO was migrated into the new SAM portal.

The FedBizOpps migration into SAM was bumpy to say the least. As of early 2020, the majority of government contractors are still frustrated with the lack of functionality in SAM. So, whether you are new to government sales or you've been selling to the government for years, we are all working through the challenges. We know that the Federal Procurement Data

---

[2] IAE environment metrics as outlined by GSA on the IAE landing page www.gsa.gov/iae

System (FPDS) will be migrated in 'blocks.' I'm assuming that the same is taking place with FedBizOpps functionality.

Wage determinations (WDs) and FedBizOpps have been migrated into the Integrated Award Environment (IAE) and the Past Performance Information Retrieval System, or PPIRS, has been migrated into the Contractor Performance Assessment Reporting System (CPARS). It looks like CPARS will be integrated into the IAE as one of the final system migrations.

FedBizOpps and its migration into SAM is an extremely important migration. It's how government contractors find opportunities to bid on.

Just as important is government contract data that currently resides in the Federal Procurement Data System (FPDS). FPDS is where you go to identify 'Propensity."[3] Propensity is defined as: *Who buys what you sell, how much they buy, and how often they buy it.* The migration of FPDS into SAM is taking place throughout 2020. It'll be deployed in 'blocks' of functionality.

I am one of several hundred FPDS power-users that GSA contacted to test-drive the new ad-hoc search functionality within the SAM testing environment. Visit my LinkedIn profile for an article I wrote on the upcoming changes to FPDS and its migration into the SAM / IAE environment. I'll be providing feedback on my testing and other updates.

There are many other system updates and changes but these are the big ones so far. Expect more.

DUNS to SAMMI

If you want to better understand DUNS versus SAMMI versus CAGE code, then you'll find this piece interesting. This section is a combination of known facts sprinkled with a bit of deduction.

If you're already registered in the System for Award Management (SAM), you know your DUNS number. Every company has one or more

---

[3] Propensity, defined as "who buys what you sell, how much they buy, and how often they buy it" was coined by the author in 2008.

DUNS numbers. Most small to mid-sized companies have one. Larger companies often have more than one for various reasons.

However, companies have one *Global DUNS Number.* In federal acquisition, DUNS is a unique identifier for government contractors.

In 1963, Dun and Bradstreet (D&B) introduced the DUNS number to support its credit reporting services. It is now a worldwide standard. DUNS stands-for Data Universal Numbering System.

So, for more than 50 years, Dun and Bradstreet (D&B) has owned the market for universal data numbering to identify specific entities and companies. The US Government has been using the DUNS number as a unique identifier since the late 1980s. [4]

In 2019, the General Services Administration (GSA) awarded Ernst and Young LLP (EY) a five-year $42 million contract for the US Government to take control of unique identifiers and create a *non-proprietary* unique identifier.

This is interesting from a business perspective. Not only will Dun and Bradstreet lose millions of dollars, the US Government, for the first time in 30 years, has chosen to make the unique identifier a government identifier versus an industry proprietary identifier. Sure, the government has the right to change from DUNS to SAMMI, but after 30 years and for lack of a better term, you can't help but draw comparisons to eminent domain. That said, I agree with the decision. From both a technology and business perspective, it makes sense.

By the end of 2020, under a five-year contract with Ernst and Young, the DUNS number will be replaced by the System for Award Management – Managed Identifier (SAMMI).

Similar to how your DUNS number is directly associated with your legal business name, the SAMMI number will be associated with your legal business name, doing business as (dba) names, and address. Theoretically, it should be easier for the government to manage SAMMI numbers versus having to deal with a contractor.

---

[4] Federal Register 26470, May 5, 2006

We don't yet know how the migration from DUNS to SAMMI will take place. We know that it will directly impact almost **EVERY government system** as well as **EVERY government contractor**.

Every government system; every contract action; every awarded contract will have to map the old DUNS number to the new SAMMI number. While SAMMI is the future, there are millions of contracts where the unique identifier is DUNS. As a result, all past, historical, and current contracts must be mapped for *BOTH DUNS and SAMMI*. There are 80 data systems in the federal government that contain DUNS information. That's a lot of systems! Every system must rekey every contract action to use SAMMI as the unique identifier. This is a massive undertaking with extensive testing. If it were easy, the process wouldn't cost $42 million dollars.

One of the issues with a DUNS number is the methodology of how Dun and Bradstreet (D&B) establishes corporate ownership. How D&B established ownership for a company is different from how DLA establishes ownership via Commercial and Government Entity (CAGE) System Codes. In some respects, CAGE codes present a more accurate picture of a company's ownership.

CAGE codes are also used for geographical identification. For example, Lockheed Martin, a multi-billion-dollar Defense contractor, has 900 CAGE Codes. Each code represents a specific geographical location. Most small businesses have one office location so only one CAGE code.

In 2014, an executive branch-wide requirement for prospective contractors to obtain a CAGE code was established. Any contract awarded above the micro-purchase threshold required that the contractor have a CAGE code prior to award. [5]

Today, you automatically obtain a CAGE code when you register in the System for Award Management (SAM).

The CAGE Branch for the Defense Logistics Agency (DLA), where CAGE codes are assigned and the program is managed, was considered a possible replacement for the DUNS number. With extensive discussions in

---

[5] Unique Identification Codes for Federal Contractors: DUNS Numbers and CAGE Codes; Congressional Research Service; November 21, 2016 (R44490)

Congress and with GSA stating publicly that Dun and Bradstreet's DUNS number was a de-facto monopoly, CAGE codes took on a new role. Since 2014 the government has been accelerating use of CAGE codes in parallel with discussions for possible transition of the DUNS number to a non-proprietary identifier.

Even so, CAGE codes did not replace the DUNS number. The SAM Managed Identifier (SAMMI) replaced the DUNS number.

Many contractors provide services so the DUNS number is their primary focus. But there are also billions of dollars spent through procurement systems such as the Defense Logistics Agency's (DLA) Internet Bid Board System (DIBBS). For most contractors using DIBBS (as well as government buyers), the CAGE code is their critical focal point - as that's how authorized manufacturers, resellers, distributors and how products are tracked.

So, we have SAMMI replacing the DUNS number… but where does the CAGE code fit into all of this? Well… it's not replacing DUNS.

My intent is not to confuse you. I can only assume that CAGE Branch at DLA is supporting the DUNS to SAMMI migration (in some fashion). If not, then from a common sense perspective, we (that's me and the mouse in my pocket) can assume that the purpose and use of CAGE codes will see major shifts in the coming years. We'll find out more as SAMMI codes are deployed.

If you're a government contractor, recommend using both your DUNS and SAMMI numbers on your marketing, business card, capability statement, website, and proposals for the first year or two after SAMMI numbers are instituted. We'll know more when GSA launches the new identifier.

New GSA Consolidated Schedule

The GSA Schedule program is one of the flagship acquisition mechanisms for the U.S. Government. GSA Schedules are just one acquisition mechanism for selling to the government. Of the 600,000+ companies registered in the System for Award Management (SAM), only ~20,000 have a GSA Schedule. If you know how to properly use a schedule, you can make some good money. Some companies make millions or billions of dollars on their GSA Schedule. 50% of companies that have a schedule fail to successfully win a contract.

Step back and think about what I just said. 50% of GSA Schedule holders fail to win government contracts.[6]

That's crazy! It's also reality.

Let me go off on a tangent. Why do 50% of companies fail to successfully use their GSA Schedule? The answers are woven throughout this book.

It's not what you know. It's not what you learn. *It's how you apply it.* But I digress. We'll cover this throughout the book.

Industry FAQ from GSA's Website [7]

The Multiple Award Schedules (MAS) Consolidation initiative is one of four cornerstone projects underpinning GSA's Federal Marketplace Strategy (FMP) to modernize and simplify the buying and selling experience for customers, suppliers and acquisition professionals.

GSA is modernizing federal acquisition by consolidating the existing 24 Schedules into one single Schedule for products, services, and solutions. This provides consistency in the program for all stakeholders, makes it easier for customers to find total solutions under one contract vehicle, ensures terms and conditions to meet the needs of our customers, and eliminates duplicate contracts.

---

[6] From RSM Federal research in 2018 where 50% of companies made less than $25,000 on their GSA Schedule. Of these 10,000 companies, 7,000 didn't make a single penny. The other 3,000 companies made less than $25,000. However, failure to make $25,000 will trigger loss of a company's schedule.

[7] https://www.gsa.gov/buying-selling/purchasing-programs/gsa-schedules/schedules-news-and-updates

If you currently have a GSA Schedule, you will be asked to migrate your schedule to the new consolidated schedule sometime in 2020 (or possibly 2021).

One of the most common frustrations for contractors as well as the government has been a lack of standardization on schedules. Not only is the government working to remove duplication of product and services, GSA also wants to standardize the terms and conditions for delivery, price, and trade agreements.

To be clear, this is also an opportunity to bring GSA Schedules under the best practices of **category management** which we'll discuss in Chapter 7. What I really like about the new consolidated schedule is that companies will no longer need to have two, three, or even four different GSA Schedules; all managed by different GSA contracting officers; all requiring monthly reporting and Industrial Funding Fee (IFF) requirements.

The solicitation for the new consolidated GSA Schedule was released in calendar quarter Q4 of 2019. If you want a GSA Schedule and you don't currently have one, you will start by finding the consolidated schedule on SAM. There are no longer 24 different solicitations on SAM. Just one.

Note. If you're interested in obtaining a GSA Schedule, I developed a step-by-step process for *validating if you really need one*. It's one of the many resources in the Federal Access Knowledge-Base. (https://rsmfederal.com/FA)

For current GSA Schedule holders, you'll be contacted by your contracting officer when they are ready for you to start migrating to the consolidated schedule, probably sometime in 2020.

There are many other changes taking place to government systems. We've seen more changes, major changes, in the last 24 months than we've seen in decades. As the government continues to modernize their systems, how are you going to keep on top of these changes? Will you be reactive and worried when you're surprised with an update? Or will keeping tabs on these updates be a part of your general business strategy?

You can always connect with me on LinkedIn to make sure you don't lose sight or track of these updates.

Something to think about.

Chapter 3.
Your Value In 45 Seconds

This is probably one of my most popular strategies. It is used by thousands of companies, various PTACs, and quite a few small business counselors and consultants.

Think about the last conference you attended. You were walking around the exhibit hall and someone approached you and said, "Hi! I'm Janice. What do you do?"

Most business developers and business owners respond in a similar manner. We do what we were taught. It is common practice for small companies to believe their certifications are more important than their products or services. For many, even though they understand that their products and services are more important, they still fail to position properly. Many companies respond with:

- Hi! We are a woman-owned small business (WOSB) that provides technology services; or

- We are an 8a (minority or socially disadvantaged), veteran-owned electrical contractor; or

- I am with ABC Construction and we are a small business that provides vertical construction services; or

- I am with XYZ Environmental, a small business that provides environmental services.

There are several problems with these responses. First, they do not communicate value. Furthermore, if you introduce yourself as small business, 8(a), woman owned, veteran, or any other status, *you are telling me that you believe the value of your company is your status* and not the value of your products and services.

Tens of thousands of small businesses do this every day. Think about this for a minute!

This runs against many basic business principles. The next time you are told to put your certification "front and center," understand that this advice is based on federal and congressional small-business mandates and regulations. This guidance does not necessarily take into account the tenets of general business strategy.

Your certifications *will always come-out during discussion*. That is the nature of working in the government market. Just because there are 23%, 5%, or 3% set-aside requirements, is not enough reason for me to buy from you or team with your company.

You are not a status. You are a company that provides value.

In 45 seconds, you need to accomplish three things.

First, you need to communicate your value. Not your small business status and not what you sell. Do not tell me that you are a small business; that you are 8(a) or woman-owned. Do not simply tell me what products or services you sell.

I want you to tell me the value that your products or services provide to your customers.

Second, you need to communicate proof. I just met you. I don't know you. You can tell me about your products and services, but I am still questioning the maturity of your business. Why shouldn't I? You are the thirty-fifth small business I have spoken to today that provides these capabilities. You need to provide examples of your past performance to create a perception that you have the necessary experience.

Every company thinks they provide amazing value. This is a pre-requisite to corporate growth. It's part philosophy and part culture. You have to think this way. But I have not seen all those great testimonials on your website (*and you have not given me a reason to go look*).

After you outline the value that your company provides, you need to convince me in 5 seconds that you are a mature business. This applies even if you are a one-person company. You need to convince me that you not only know what you are doing, but that you are good at it.

Third, you need to differentiate yourself from all the other companies I have been talking to. You do this my *making yourself equal to your competition before you differentiate.*

Value. Proof. Differentiate.

Let me give you an example so you can apply this to your business. When you read this 45 second pitch, you will not hear me say that I am small, woman, or veteran owned. Also notice, I do not say I am a technology company.

Read this and watch how I transition from value to proof to differentiation:

"We are in the business of streamlining and consolidating information and data across multiple dispersed networks to increase the visibility, accuracy, and speed of access across the enterprise. On average, we save our clients ~ 30% in operational expenses and a more than 25% savings in data integrity and database cleansing costs. We have provided these benefits to Monsanto, Blue Cross - Blue Shield, and the US Army Corps of Engineers (USACE). Like most companies in our space, our website and marketing collateral list half a dozen products or services, but the two products (or services) that provide the most value to our customers are A and B...

Okay, the value statements clearly identify the type of company we are and the services we provide. The value statements were 30% savings in operational expenses and 25% savings in data integrity costs. I also spoke about visibility, accuracy, and speed of access. It is obvious we are a technology company (even though I didn't say it).

On a side note, yes, it is okay to say you are a technology company. My point is that you should be able communicate what you do by allowing your value to communicate it for you!

If I introduce myself to you in this manner and then immediately follow-up with a short list of clients, such as Monsanto, Blue Cross, and the Army Corps of Engineers, you are immediately thinking, "Okay, they have past performance. They have experience. They did not open for business yesterday."

And then I want to make absolutely sure that I do not sound like other companies. I explain that even though our website and capability statement may outline the same products and services as everyone else, we really excel and *provide extensive value* in *two core areas.*

I just made myself equal to the competition and then I differentiated by outlining the two products or services that we specialize in; the two capabilities that set-us apart.

When I use this technique, depending on who I am talking to, *I change the two core capabilities.* Why would I change them? Perhaps I just spent an hour meeting with a prospect. I now understand what they are looking for. I now have a better understanding of their requirements and their challenges. If I know she is looking for one or two specific capabilities, I am going to market and position for those two moving forward.

If you gave this 45 second pitch to me, I would be thinking, "Finally! A company that doesn't think they do it all! This sounds like a quality and mature business that understands their strengths and capabilities."

It is about positioning. It is about marketing. It is about perception.

It is about combining your understanding of government procurement with *business strategy.* What is exciting about this strategy is that once you have figured out how to communicate your value, you will have transformed how you market to the government. Better yet, this strategy, like most of the strategies in this book, are market agnostic. This will provide value as well when you are engaging commercial opportunities.

Not only will you have a solid sales pitch, you will also be able to use this information to update your website and capability statement.

Value. Proof. Differentiation. All in 45 seconds.

How are you going to change your approach?

Something to think about.

Chapter 4.
Ghosting Requirements
and Influencing the Acquisition

I t would be difficult to outline the strategies and examples that I provide in several months of training and coaching. However, *this chapter is one of the more important and valuable of the strategies in this book.*

Since the launch of this book a year ago, every time I speak at a national event at least a couple folks walk up and say, "We're ghosting!" Little did I know that when I termed 'ghosting' from a business perspective that it would become one of the most recognizable business strategies that I coach.

Every chapter in this book provides important case studies and recommendations for common challenges in government sales. Ghosting is one of the most valuable strategies you can learn. In addition to what I cover in this chapter, there is a full on-demand webinar for *Responding to a Sources-Sought and Influencing the Acquisition.* If after reading this chapter you decide you want to improve your understanding even more, I strongly recommend you watch the video. You will find it at https://rsmfederal.com in our products section.

For this chapter, I have chosen to use responding to a sources-sought because it is one of the easiest ways to understand ghosting.

If you have seen me at a conference, heard a podcast, or been at one of my events, you have heard me use the phrase '*ghosting requirements and influencing the acquisition.*"

This is one of most powerful concepts that I teach business owners, sales professionals, and proposal managers. This chapter is packed with so many concepts and strategies that I recommend you grab a highlighter before you read any further.

Now, take a step back. I want you to think about some of the request for proposals (RFP) you have read. How many times have you reviewed an RFP or RFQ, recognized it was for exactly what you sell and then with a shake of your head you ditch it and move to the next opportunity?

How many times have you looked at an RFP and said to yourself, "This is a 'wired' contract. The past performance or other requirements look like they were written for a specific company." You and many other companies decide to skip it and move to other opportunities.

This does not magically happen. When you see a procurement that is 'wired' for another company it is because someone else *ghosted requirements in order to influence the acquisition and marginalize the competition.*

Sometimes a procurement is so obviously written for another company that all you can do is shake your head and move on. Other times, you will bid and still have a chance at winning.

Companies that understand how to "ghost requirements" will increase their competitiveness in the market. This isn't theoretical. Ghosting is one of the reasons our clients went from $2 billion to $2.6 billion in government contracts – just last year.

The objective of this chapter is for you to understand the concept of ghosting and start doing it yourself!

Ghosting Defined

This is one of the most enjoyable and valuable concepts for the companies that I coach. It is based on the general business principle of positioning a company's value inside the prospect's decision cycle in order to influence an acquisition.

I am going to provide the basics of ghosting so that you understand its value.

Let's start with a definition for Ghosting. NOTE [8]:

---

[8] "Ghosting Requirements" (coined by the author) and Influencing the Acquisition, with its associated definitions, was developed by Joshua Frank in 2001

26

- Ghosting is positioning the *value* of your capabilities and differentiators in order to **marginalize your competition**.

- Ghosting is an activity you perform in order to **bar-entry or decrease the perceived effectiveness** of your competition.

- Ghosting is a process of taking your competition's weaknesses, tailoring your competencies to compensate, and positioning your strengths to **build a competitive advantage**.

- Ghosting is a process where you **recommend information and value** that you want to have included in the RFP or RFQ. You do this in order to provide your company with a competitive advantage.

Now, if we boil this down, there are two types of ghosting.

- Positioning your value, capabilities, differentiators, and past performance to marginalize your competition.

- Positioning your competition's weaknesses though your strengths.

Acquisition vs. Pre-Acquisition

Next, we need to define Acquisition versus Pre-Acquisition. Pre-acquisition is simply the time period before an RFP or RFQ is released for competition. Examples include sources-sought, draft-solicitations, pre-solicitations, and building relationships with your government prospects *without regard to any specific opportunity*.

Once a procurement is released (whether it is on SAM, GSA eBuy, DIBBS, FedMall, or any other government system) it has moved into the acquisition phase.

It is critically important that you understand the difference between acquisition and pre-acquisition. 80% of every week should be focused on pre-acquisition activities! I will discuss this more in later chapters.

---

as part of coaching companies on how to position for and win government contracts.

If this sounds complicated, it may at first. But like anything else, you simply need someone to show you how to do it. For you to successfully ghost a requirement and influence an acquisition, you need to have:

- a strong understanding of the market;

- a strong understanding of the prospect;

- a strong understanding of how to communicate the value of your products and services;

- a strong understanding of your competition's weaknesses; and

- the ability to strategically position with the prospect

Yes, sometimes the government will know what you are doing. They may not call it ghosting, but they will recognize that you are attempting to influence their acquisition strategy. Even if they recognize what you are doing, as long as you are ghosting correctly, not only will they not care, but you will have a good chance of influencing the procurement.

So, before we dive into some examples of ghosting, we need a little more background. Let's discuss some of the basics for responding to a sources-sought.

Sources-Sought

A sources-sought is an acquisition mechanism for market research to validate if the small business community is capable of supporting a set of requirements. Market research includes, but is not limited to:

- corporate background

- a vendor's technical capabilities

- relevant experience (past performance)

- applicable industry certifications

- investments in quality and process

Since we know that the government uses sources-sought to facilitate acquisition strategy and we know that sources-sought fall under pre-acquisition, this is an *excellent opportunity* to ghost requirements and attempt to influence the procurement.

Going off on a quick tangent - last year, more than $20 billion went to large companies because small businesses failed to respond to sources-sought. I have spoken to hundreds of contracting officers and they all say the same thing. "Small businesses constantly ask us to set-aside procurements but then no one responds to our sources-sought."

$20 billion tagged for small business and went to large companies.

If you see a sources-sought, *do not assume* that other small businesses are going to respond! Yes, I know, you have a lot going on. You are working on a proposal. You are dealing with an employee issue. But you cannot assume other companies are responding. Also, when you respond to a sources-sought, let one or two other small businesses know that they should respond as well.

Asking other companies to respond? Yes. I know this goes against common business paradigms for competition and protecting your competitive position in the market, but the contracting officer requires *at least two responses* to conclude that the small business community is capable of fulfilling the requirements. If you are the only one to respond, guess what? It will be a full and open competition and now you will be competing against large companies. When you use this strategy, look for other companies that can support the requirements but are *less mature or capable than your company*. Those are the companies you ask to send in a response.

Your objective in responding to a sources sought is to influence the acquisition. That is it! There is no contract to win at this stage. You are focused on influencing the acquisition. The one exception would be for 8a firms (minority and socially disadvantaged) where the majority of sole-source awards are made. But even if you are 8a, your primary objective is not getting a sole-source award. *It is to influence the acquisition.* Of course, to influence the acquisition, one of your ghosted recommendations could be to sole-source to your company.

This is not semantics. Your primary objective is to influence the acquisition. If you have "sole-source on the brain," you will be primarily focused on sole-source when you should be focused on ghosting other requirements. If the government does not sole-source, now what do you do? If you did not ghost any other requirements, you will have failed to influence your competitiveness.

Your Socio-Economic Status

For 8a firms, sole-source awards do not happen magically or automatically. They do not fall-off trees and they are not easy to obtain. Whether you are 8a or any other socio-economic status (woman-owned, veteran-owned, etc.) *you do not win contracts because of your status*. You win contracts because of the *value* you provide. This means that leading with your status on your capability statement, on your website, and when you introduce yourself to prospects does not make smart business sense. As discussed in the previous chapter, you should not start with, "Hi, my name is Mary and we are a woman-owned, veteran-owned small business that sells vertical construction services."

To emphasize this point, if you are certified 8a by the Small Business Administration (SBA), you are not going to win a sole-sole award *or any award* because you are 8a. You will win a contract because you have proven that your products or services provide outstanding value.

So, if you follow the business logic, it is no different than competing on any other procurement. Your socio-economic status opens doors. *It does not win you contracts*. This goes against much of the guidance you receive in the market today. Yes... I'm telling you that some of the guidance you've received from others violates basic business strategy.

When I present the seminar on "How To Successfully Take Advantage of Your Socio-Economic Status," attendees look at me like I'm abusing a puppy.

Yes, the federal government has a 23% goal for small business; 5% for 8a; 5% for woman-owned; 3% for service-disabled veteran-owned; and 3% for HUBZone. Notice that I did not list veteran-owned. That is because there is no mandated percentage for veteran-owned companies, just service-disabled. (If you are veteran-owned, you need to identify the top agencies or military commands that have extensive veteran-owned procurements. Hint - the Department of Veterans Affairs is a likely target.)

Consider any set-aside procurement. Imagine for a moment there is a procurement for an environmental audit and remediation. Assume you have successfully influenced the acquisition and it is released as a set-aside for woman-owned small business (WOSB). Congratulations. Now ask yourself this question, "If 27 companies respond to the RFP, what socio-economic status will they all have?"

Correct - every company is a woman-owned small business (WOSB).

Now, which company is going to win? The one that yells from the mountain-top that they are woman-owned and the government has a 5% mandate to use their services? Or the company that 'softly' communicates its socio-economic status, leads with and *focuses on the value they provide*?

This is when the light-bulbs go off across the room. You do not win contracts because of your status or certifications. That is a misnomer that goes against basic business principles. Yes, being a small business and having other small business certifications will open doors for you, but you win because you communicate stronger value.

You are not a status! You are a company that provides value.

This is how you *must* approach the market. This is how small businesses become big businesses.

Again, I know this goes against common market guidance. Everyone has told you, "Hey! The government has all these mandated percentages! You need to put your status front and center! They are looking for companies just like yours!"

All of this is true. But how you position in the market will make or break your company. Failing to understand the concept of "softly communicating your status" is why small businesses fail to win government contracts.

NAICS Code Not Required for Award?

I am going to go off on another tangent. The government will often have a tentative NAICS code identified for the procurement in the sources-sought. NAICS stands for North American Industrial Classification System. Before you respond to a sources-sought (or any bid, RFP, or RFQ), make sure that the NAICS code is in your System for Award Management (SAM) profile. You might as well do it now and not forget to do it when you submit a proposal.)

An interesting point on NAICS codes. During final review and edits before the first edition of this book was published, one of the reviewers forwarded an article by Matthew Schoonover, Managing Partner at Koprince Law LLC. The article referenced a Government Accountability Office (GAO) decision (Veterans Electric, LLC, B-413198 (Aug. 26, 2016)) where it was found that an awardee is *not required* to list the specified NAICS code in their System for Award Management (SAM) profile.

An electrical contractor, Architecture Consulting Group (ACG) won a contract but did not have the NAICS code listed in their SAM profile. The GAO upheld their contract for several reasons. I will not go into the specifics of the case, but there is now precedence where GAO will not sustain a protest based on a failure of the awardee to list the acquisition's NAICS code in their SAM profile.

Seems clear cut, right? It is not.

Like many findings in the government market, just because there appears to be law, regulation, or finding, does not mean that the market is abiding by that regulation or that the market is even aware of it.

Here is a perfect case in point: The United States Supreme Court found that the Department of Veterans Affairs (VA) was wrong to ignore the "rule of two" after the VA had met their small business and veteran goals. In a well-known case, the company Kingdomware protested an award to the Government Accountability Office (GAO). The GAO upheld the protest, saying that the VA should have followed the rule of two. The VA disagreed with the GAO's findings and *declined to follow the GAO's recommendation*.

When the VA declined to follow the GAO's guidance, the case was accepted by the United States Supreme Court. In a landmark decision, the highest court in the land ruled that the VA must award to a veteran-owned concern when two or more veteran-owned business were capable of performing the contract - even after meeting its small business and veteran-owned percentages.

But even after the Supreme Court decision, it is well documented that various VA contracting offices continued to drag their feet.

My point - even when there is a regulation or law, the government is no different than corporate America. Do not assume that government contracting officers are aware of the regulation or that they will proactively follow-it.

Second, GAO decisions are non-binding. That means just because the GAO makes a finding on the listing or non-listing of NAICS codes in a SAM profile, does not imply the agency or military command must follow it.

Third, you should not assume that the acquisition community recognizes the implications. For all these reasons, yes, if you do not have the procurement's NAICS code in your SAM profile, you can still win the contract.

However, *from a business perspective*, which would you prefer? Spending two weeks and potentially thousands of dollars defending against a protest (regardless of the GAOs decision on NAICS codes) or taking ten minutes to validate that the NAICS code is in your SAM profile?

Business is not black and white. Add to this that government acquisition strategy is changing faster than I can type this sentence. Regardless of the GAO decision on NAICS codes, do not lose sight of the operational and opportunity-costs. Make sure you have the NAICS code listed in your SAM profile.

Responding to a Sources-Sought

Back to our discussion on ghosting recommendations in a sources-sought. A sources-sought helps the government facilitate their acquisition strategy. The most common objective is to validate if the procurement should be full and open, set-aside for small business, or for one of the socio-economic statuses.

A sources-sought is an excellent opportunity to position and influence before the RFP or RFQ is released. Have you ever looked at a sources-sought and asked yourself, "What would I like to see in the RFP?" Or do you simply respond to the questions the government asks you? Most companies simply respond to the questions.

You should never respond to a sources-sought without ghosting requirements. Ever. Ever ever.

In other words, *you will always give the government more* than what they asked for in your sources-sought response. What requirements would you like to see in the RFP? Which requirements would allow you to have a stronger competitive advantage over your competition? Which competition weaknesses would you like to ghost into the RFP's statement of work (SOW) or performance work statement (PWS)?

Stay with me… I need to outline several more concepts before we move to examples. It is critical that you understand how to approach a sources-sought before you start ghosting.

The next several points will fly in the face of industry guidance. There are quite a few industry experts that tell a sources-sought is not the time to get creative. Simply give the government what they are asking for. At the same time, they tell you that you can use a sources-sought to influence the procurement.

Now hold on. How are you supposed to simply answer their questions, not be creative, and then successfully influence the acquisition? That makes no sense. Think about this for a minute. Here are several points I want you to consider the next time you respond to a sources-sought.

First, You do not have to answer every question. This is so misunderstood by the small business community that I drill this into every seminar and training event. If you respond to an RFP and your proposal fails to respond to key requirements in the statement of work, you are what is called 'non-responsive.' If source-selection finds your proposal to be non-responsive (because you forgot to discuss certain requirements), you are removed from competition.

Well guess what? A sources-sought does not follow the same regulations. *It is impossible for you to be non-responsive on a sources sought.* You do not win any money on a sources-sought and the government is not obligating funds. It is simply market research.

If you feel that answering a question will not be advantageous to your positioning, then *do not answer the question.*

You and the government have conflicting priorities and objectives on a sources-sought. The government wants everything they can get from you in order to make a stronger decision on a future acquisition strategy. *Your objective is to influence the acquisition.*

At almost every national and major event, a contracting officer comes up after a seminar to discuss my strategies. At the last conference, a contracting officer from the Department of Homeland Security (DHS) took me aside and said:

"Man, I don't think I have ever seen a training session like that. I was expecting the same generic B.S. that everyone else preaches. Part of me is frustrated with your

recommendations to small business because your strategies will make my job harder. But the other half recognizes that what you coach makes perfect sense. I totally get it from a business perspective. Well done."

When you respond to a sources-sought, you are doing one of two things. You are either validating the government's acquisition strategy or *you are changing it*. How do you change it?

You ghost requirements.

Here is another point to consider when you respond to your next sources-sought. I want you to think of a sources-sought as a negotiation. They want everything you have. But if you do not want to provide something, then don't. Do not explain why you skipped a question. Simply do not include that question in your response.

Also, make sure you CC or send a copy of your response to the small business office for that agency or military command.

The final point I want to make is about the deadline for turning-in your response. With a show-of-hands, have you ever seen a sources-sought and realized it was due several days earlier? (If you ever see me at a conference, tell me you raised your hand while reading my book... we'll have a good laugh!)

For most small businesses, missing sources-sought responses is a monthly occurrence. An owner or business developer will miss it and then what do they do? They make an entry on the pipeline that the opportunity had a sources-sought, that they missed it, but to be on the look-out for the RFP.

The problem is that you just missed a major opportunity to ghost requirements. You've just missed an opportunity to influence the acquisition, right?

Wrong. You did not miss an opportunity.

Unlike responses to RFPs in the acquisition phase, *sources-sought are pre-acquisition*. As a result, the timelines and suspense dates provided by the government are not legally locked in stone like an RFP.

If you missed the suspense date for turning in your sources-sought response, *you can still turn it in*. Seventy to eighty percent of the time, you will simply get an email back from the contracting officer saying, "Got it. Thanks!"

The government contracting officer wants small businesses to respond. What if there had only been one response? They need a minimum of two! You may have been the second response. Also, they want your feedback. Since the regulations do not prohibit them from accepting a response after the due-date, why not?

Assuming the agency is not moving from a sources-sought response directly into acquisition (releasing an RFP or RFQ), you could respond up to a week or two after the suspense date! I have seen the government confirm receipt of a response four weeks after the due date. But that is really pushing it. *Do not make a practice of this.* If you are constantly missing sources-sought deadlines, then you need to look at your internal process. But if it is a perfect opportunity and you know your company would be competitive, then respond.

Bottom line, just because you missed a response date on a sources-sought does not mean you can't respond!

To this point, we have defined ghosting, discussed the differences between acquisition and pre-acquisition, the importance of 'softly' communicating your socio-economic status, and several recommendations on responding to a sources sought.

So, what can you ghost and how does it work?

Ghosting Requirements

You can ghost anything. Here is a list of common items that you should consider ghosting in your sources sought-response:

- Acquisition Size – Should the acquisition be full and open (large companies can compete) or a small business set-aside?

- Socio-Economic Status – Should the set-aside be for small business, woman-owned, 8a, veteran-owned, service-disabled veteran-owned, HUBZone, etc.?

- Acquisition Codes – Which North American Industrial Classification System (NAICS) code should be utilized on the acquisition?

- Contract Vehicles – Should the procurement be released open-market, on GSA Schedule, on an existing blanket purchase agreement (BPA), or on an agency or government-wide contract vehicle? If you are a prime or subcontractor on an existing indefinite delivery indefinite quantity (IDIQ) contract, do you want to push the government to use that vehicle?

- Your Strengths and what differentiates you

- The Weakness of your competition

- Certifications – Includes individual employee certifications and company certifications.

- Security – Do any employees have active security clearances? Does the company have a facility clearance?

- Your Past Performance

- Quality – Does your company have a strong quality assurance (QA) or quality control (QC) plan?

- You can ghost anything

Ghosting Is When You Reverse the Direction of Information and Value

When most business professionals think of business intelligence, they think of information that is not publicly available, that will provide them with a competitive advantage during the proposal phase. This is absolutely right. This is how you differentiate and position to communicate stronger value than your competition.

But business intelligence *goes both ways*! When you are responding to a sources-sought, having a face-to-face meeting with a government prospect, or meeting with a potential teaming partner, you are not only pulling intelligence, you are also pushing information as well.

You are pushing information that will help the government write stronger requirements. You are pushing information that alerts the government to certain challenges or risks if they do not consider changing or updating their current plan.

You are ghosting requirements.

Examples of Ghosting

Because every agency and opportunity are different, you should ghost different requirements for every opportunity you engage. What you ghost is dependent on your past performance, your capabilities, your value, your employees, and the government's current requirements.

Ghosting requirements to influence an acquisition is no different than responding to an RFP or RFQ. Every response will be different and you have to tailor your recommendations.

I have chosen four real-world scenarios to help you better understand ghosting. Remember, you can ghost anything. That means there are hundreds of examples I could choose from. I've chosen to discuss four that lend themselves to an easier understanding of the strategy.

#1. Acquisition Codes

Requests for proposal (RFP) and Requests for quote (RFQ) are released under a North American Industrial Classification System (NAICS) code. If you have operated in the government market for even a month, you know your codes. If you are new to government sales, reach out to your local procurement technical assistance center (PTAC) and they will show you how to find your codes.

Many companies use their NAICS codes as the primary search criteria for finding opportunities. Going off on another tangent, the best way to search for opportunities is actually by using Product Service Codes (PSC) which are more granular. Many companies say, "Ugh! When I search by our NAICS codes, I get hundreds of results and very few of them are for what we do." This is not unusual. It does not always work but every company should try searching by PSC codes. Also, I never recommend that you only search by NAICS or PSC codes. I recommend a combination of codes and *keywords*.

What if an agency released a procurement under the wrong code? What do you think will happen? Very few of the companies that would bid on the opportunity *will actually see it*. If the code does not change, fewer companies will be aware of it. There will be fewer companies that bid on it.

Additionally, do you remember when you first identified your NAICS codes and entered them into the System for Award Management (SAM)? Did anyone verify that you actually sell those products or services? No. You can add, delete, or change your NAICS codes every day if you wanted to. My point is that if you find an opportunity for what you sell but it is under a NAICS code you do not have, just go into SAM and add it. This is not ghosting. This is just a day in the life of a government contractor. Once you have the right codes, you probably will not be changing them anyway.

One form of ghosting is asking the government to maintain or change the NAICS code. Sometimes the NAICS code selected by the government is just the wrong code. Sometimes they accidentally use a product code instead of a service code. There are many reasons why there could be a wrong code.

Many consultants and small business advisors will instruct you to recommend one of your codes if you do not have the NAICS code listed in the sources-sought. While I concur with this recommendation, this is easy and may or may not influence the acquisition. First, if the government does not change the code, all you have to do is add it to your SAM profile. If they do change the code to one of your codes, you are not necessarily going to marginalize or bar-entry to your competition.

When it comes to ghosting acquisition codes, I want you to ask yourself two questions.

- In searching USASpending.gov or the Federal Procurement Data System (Soon to be integrated into the Integrated Award Environment (IAE) / System for Award Management (SAM)), what are the top two or three NAICS codes used to buy the products you sell or the services you provide?

- What are the small business size standards for each of these NAICS codes?

As an example, let's say you are a graphical design firm that generates $1.5 million in revenue. Your primary NAICS code is 541430. This code falls under the umbrella of subsector 541 – Professional, Scientific, and Technical Services. If you are an information technology (IT) firm, you are in the 541 NAICS code sector.

Even though graphical design services are acquired under 541430, you are smart enough to have weekly searches on the other NAICS codes in the

541 family. One day you are reviewing opportunities and a key-word search finds a sources-sought for graphical design services. Not only is it exactly what your company provides, but you have excellent past performance within the last three years.

The sources-sought currently identifies the NAICS code as 541519 for Other Computer Related Services. Now, even though 541430 (graphical design) is your primary NAICS code, you also have 541519 in your SAM profile.

What do most companies do? They simply check a box. "Yep, that is one of our codes. We're good!"

Here is the problem. Many information technology firms have in-house graphical designers. You are not just competing with graphical design companies. You are also competing with larger and more mature technology firms.

Let's look at the Small Business Administration (SBA) size standards for these NAICS codes. NOTE [9]

- 541519 has a size standard of $30,00,000

- 541430 has a size standard of $8,000,000

This is one of best examples for understanding the concept of ghosting. There will be more companies that qualify as small business under 541519. Not only will there be more companies, they will be more mature and smaller companies. They will be larger. They will likely have more or possibly stronger past performance.

Remember, one of the objectives for ghosting is to *bar-entry* to your competition.

By getting the government to change the code to 541430, the only companies that can bid on this graphical design contract are now under $8 million.

---

[9] As of August 19, 2019, Table of Small Business Size Standards Matched to North American Industry Classification System Codes, Small Business Administration. https://www.sba.gov/document/support--table-size-standards

You have just eliminated and barred-entry to half of your competition!

What if you are a woman-owned small business (WOSB) and the sources sought is using NAICS 541519 ($30 million)? If you convince the government that it makes more sense to procure under 541430 ($8 million) *and* they set-aside for WOSB, you have eliminated even more companies!

What if you have a GSA Schedule and you convince the government to release on schedule? Now the only companies that can bid on the opportunity are woman-owned small businesses under $8 million that have a GSA Schedule. With strong past performance you have an outstanding opportunity to win the contract.

So the next time you review a sources-sought, do not simply glance at the NAICS code and say, "Yep, we have that code." Evaluate if you can ghost a NAICS code with a *smaller size standard*.

That is ghosting. That is influencing the acquisition.

#2. Past Performance

From a complexity perspective, sources-sought fall into two categories. The government will either ask five to ten simple questions or the government wants you to complete a detailed fifteen-page questionnaire. Most are the former. The most common sources-sought asks for your company background, small business certifications, and whether you have past-performance.

When it comes to past performance, remember why the government uses a sources-sought. They want to identify if there are enough small businesses that can bid-on *and successfully perform the work*. Often-times, the government does not request that you provide specific past-performance write-ups.

Many small businesses are smart enough to include detailed past-performance sections in their sources-sought response. For companies new to government sales or companies that do not currently provided detailed past-performance sections, you need to provide *detailed* past performance write-ups that are also *tailored* to the specific requirements in the source sought.

Never respond to a sources-sought without providing two or three past-performance write-ups. It does not matter whether or not the government asks for them. Always provide them. If the government limits the number of pages to your sources-sought response and you do not have the space for past-performance write-ups, *include them anyway and exceed the authorized page count.*

I'm getting those looks again like I'm abusing a puppy. You may be thinking, "Exceed the page count? You can't do that!"

Sure you can.

Remember, as we discussed earlier in the chapter, unlike writing a proposal, your response to a sources-sought cannot fall under the threat of being non-responsive. There is nothing in the Federal Acquisition Regulation (FAR) that prevents the government from accepting a sources-sought response that exceeds the page-count. I have personally submitted hundreds of sources-sought responses that exceeded the page-count.

Almost every single time I received an email with 'thank you' from the contracting officer. I have never received an email saying, "We are not accepting your *sources-sought* because you were non-responsive and failed to follow directions on page count." Have I seen it happen? Yes, several times. Is it possible you will get a contracting officer that is being difficult? Of course. Yes, it is possible but it does not happen that often. This is one of those gray areas you need to be aware of… and take advantage of.

If you are thinking, "Well, I don't care. I am not exceeding the page count. So now what do I do?" Simple. Attach your *tailored* past performance write-ups as "Enclosure #1 - Past Performance" to your response. You could make your capability statement Enclosure 2.

Up to this point, we have not ghosted. We have simply discussed the basics of including past performance to your sources-sought response.

So, how do you ghost a past-performance and how does it make you more competitive?

There are two methods. The most common is *tailoring* your past-performance to the scope or requirements outlined in the sources-sought. When you have been in the market long enough, you will have a digital library for sources-sought and proposal responses. You will have a folder with write-ups for each of your past contracts. Most companies simply copy and paste their past-performance descriptions into their sources-sought response. Why not? It is fast and easy.

Yes, this provides the government with proof that you have past-performance. However, you should *always tailor your write-up to the scope and requirements* of the opportunity.

Always.

Everyone else is copying and pasting. You will be one of the few companies that took the time to show the government that you not only have past-performance, but that *it directly relates to their current requirements*.

The second method requires that we revisit the definition of ghosting. Ghosting is a process where you *recommend (ghost) information and value* that you want to have included in the RFP or RFQ. You do this in order to provide your company with a competitive advantage during source selection. You also do this in order to bar-entry to your competition.

The second method, recommending information and value, is used in combination with tailoring your response. To best explain how this works, let's use a real-world example. I worked with a security company in California. They installed closed-circuit television cameras (CCTV), intrusion detection (IDS) and access control systems.

When I first starting working with them, they did not have any government contracts. After getting set-up on their bid-matching tool, they found a sources-sought for a new security system at a 'federal business park' in Cincinnati, Ohio. The sources-sought identified three different buildings in need of CCTVs and access control. The security systems also had to be integrated across all three buildings.

We discussed the sources-sought and outlined how to best influence the acquisition. I asked them to call the contracting specialist and ask one simple question, "How far apart are these three buildings and are any of the buildings physically connected?"

The contracting specialist responded that two buildings were fairly close, about a hundred yards apart, separated by a road, and that the third building was in the business park, two blocks north.

We also asked the contracting specialist to provide the addresses for the three buildings. This allowed us to identify which agencies and the size of the buildings. With some additional online research, we found news articles that discussed how many federal employees worked at each location. You can often find local news articles with this type of information.

How long did it take us to collect this information? 24 hours. Yes, we did this for a sources sought! Most companies would never consider this level of effort. This also explains why many companies have such low win-rates.

First, we wanted to ensure they set it aside for small business. But we also wanted to influence the requirements. After reviewing the sources-sought and discussing what we had learned from the call with the contracting specialist, here is the section that they added to their response after answering the government's questions:

"Based on the government's description of work, we would recommend that you release this procurement as a small business set-aside. In the federal market, there are several hundred small businesses that can successfully accomplish the scope of this project. However, as this procurement is to install new security systems for three different and geographically separated buildings, supporting more than 5,000 government employees, we recommend the government consider asking for past performance that involves the complexity of integrating multiple geographically dispersed sites.

Based on our experience of deploying and maintaining security systems for major colleges, school districts, hospitals, and large corporate campuses, it is in the government's best interests for the contractor to not only have past performance, but the experience and expertise of managing and maintaining security systems across multiple locations. There are hundreds of small business security firms that have experience in wiring and maintaining systems across multiple physical sites.

Over the last several years, we have had to fix multiple installations where the previous contractor only had experience serving single locations. Asking for past performance that supports at least two interconnected buildings with integrated CCTV and access control, will likely protect the government from incurring additional costs over the next 24 months."

Now, let's take a step back and consider:

- They spoke to the government, the contracting specialist, before responding to the sources sought.

- They collected information and intelligence (location of buildings and number of federal employees) before responding.

- They ghosted "proof' of their past performance (school districts and large corporate campuses).

- They ghosted the magnitude and capability of their past performance (deployment of security systems across multiple physical sites / buildings).

- They ghosted the perception that if the government does not select a company with multiple-site experience, they are at risk of having to spend more money to resolve potential security issues.

By attempting to ghost a past performance requirement for multiple sites, they are attempting to eliminate the competitiveness of other small security companies that only have experience on smaller projects!

They are showing the government that they are not only subject matter experts with strong past performance, but they also want to ensure that the government properly scopes the requirements.

Sure, the government knows what they are doing. But that does not change the fact that the recommendation is in the best interests of the government.

If the government says, "You know... that is a good point," and asks for this type of past performance in the RFP, it will immediately make this company more competitive!

This is where the smaller security firms say, "Well darn (insert profanity). This looks like the RFP has been wired for a specific company."

That is ghosting. That is influencing the acquisition.

#3. Certifications

The next example involves ghosting of corporate or employee certifications. As discussed earlier in the chapter, I am not referring to your socio-economic status. You either convince the government to set-aside for small business or woman-owned, minority, veteran, etc. or you don't.

The type of certifications I am referring to are other corporate or employee certifications. Examples may include Cisco certifications for the technology industry. Perhaps you are in the construction field and your

45

senior managers are certified Construction Manager Certification Institute (CMCI) through the Construction Management Association of America. For large projects, you may have an employee or two that is certified Project Management Professional (PMP) via the Project Management Institute (PMI). The list is endless. Every industry has certifications.

Before starting-up RSM Federal, I worked for a company called The Newberry Group. One of the employees was given a full-time job of getting the company Capability Maturity Model Integration (CMMI) certified. At the time, the company wanted to be certified at the second maturity level. For eight months, this employee did nothing but prepare the company for certification. I have no idea what it costs today, but ten years ago it cost $75,000 in time, manpower, and cost to get certified at *each* level. Eight months later, Newberry was CMMI Level 2. Total cost - $150,000.

For the purpose of providing an example for ghosting, I will use a sources-sought from the United States Air Force that was released for software development. CMMI is a model. It is not a standard. It is sometimes required for government and Defense contracts.

One of our clients, a software development firm, had a contract with the U.S. Army. Their Army contract was to migrate a legacy system into a web-based solution. With several commercial contracts and one Army contract, they asked for recommendations on how to best position and win their first Air Force contract.

Recognizing that they must focus and engage in pre-acquisition (prior to the release of RFPs), I worked with them on engaging the prospect for six months. They built relationships with several Air Force program managers. Their focus was not on any specific opportunity. Let me say that again - *Their focus was not on any specific opportunity.*

We learned of an Air Force opportunity where the RFP had just been released. The client said, "This is really not in our wheelhouse. We will not be competitive."

I agreed that they should not respond. Then I told them to attend the industry-day for that specific RFP with the Air Force.

They just looked at me. The owner said, "Josh, I know your strategies are world class, but why on G-d's green earth should we go to the industry day if we are not going to respond to the RFP?"

I said, "Because it is the same office that released the sources-sought and the decision makers and program managers are likely to be there. When you sign-in, pay attention to what is being briefed. You never know when they will say something that provides you with intelligence. Focus on finding the program folks and wait at the door to talk to them when the event is over."

Not only did this work, but the government decision makers spoke with them about the sources-sought. The government program manager also discussed a common challenge on their projects involving detailed estimating and planning. *Remember this point because we are going to ghost this in a moment.*

Properly focused on pre-acquisition activities and building relationships, our client discussed their capabilities and identified several differentiators for ghosting. One of these was CMMI certification.

After answering all of the government's questions in the sources-sought, one of the five ghosted recommendations were for CMMI.

Here is the section they wrote to ghost CMMI:

Based on prior discussions with the Air Force Life Cycle Management Center (AFLCMC), the application development outlined in the sources-sought is similar to work we provided for the U.S. Army at XVIII Airborne Corps last year. Due to the number of systems that are directly referred to in the sources-sought and the number of systems that will be indirectly impacted by this project, we recommend that the acquisition require that the contractor have active CMMI certification and capability.

*During our work with XVIII Airborne Corps and with several of our commercial clients, the migration of legacy data to a cloud platform required extensive governance, strong decision analysis, managing performance and measurement, and **detailed estimating and planning**.*

Based on our industry expertise and previously identified challenges on a prior project with the U.S. Army, we would recommend that the Air Force incorporate CMMI level 1 or 2 to ensure maturity of vendors and their ability to successfully operate on complex projects. From an industry perspective, similar projects that fail to properly implement detailed estimating and planning cost organizations an additional 40% of initial development cost to fix and resolve.

Let's take a step back. At a high-level, let's review the set-up, activities, and what we just ghosted.

- This company spent time building relationships versus simply looking on SAM and bidding on opportunities.

- The company found a way to engage with decision makers. They attended an industry day for an *unrelated opportunity* that they had no intention of bidding on.

- During relationship building and discussions with the program manager, they learned that *estimating and planning* was a common challenge on their other projects.

- The company ghosted "proof" of their past-performance by incorporating commercial and military past-performance into their ghosted recommendation.

- They asked themselves, "We know that estimating and planning is an issue, but how do we use this to influence the acquisition?" The answer was one of their differentiators. Since two of the process areas within CMMI model's capabilities involve estimating and planning, they recommended CMMI Level 1 or 2. (Even if the government selected CMMI Level 1, they would still bar entry to non CMMI certified companies).

- They also outlined what can happen if you do not utilize CMMI during a project of 'this complexity'; e.g. 40% additional cost to resolve.

Ghosting their CMMI certification was only one of the five ghosted recommendations that they made in their sources-sought response.

Three months after submitting their response, the Air Force released the RFP. Of the five recommendations, only the one for CMMI had been added to the requirements.

The RFP actually said, "The vendor must be either CMMI Level 1 or 2."

Due to this addition, every software and technology company without CMMI certification was barred-entry to competing on the acquisition!

With a very strong proposal, our client won the contract. It was a two-year contract worth $3.5 million. It was a small-business set-aside. It was their largest contract to date.

For many small businesses, they reviewed the RFP on SAM, rolled their eyes, and mumbled about not being CMMI certified.

Ghosting is a phenomenally strong business concept. Our client did not win simply because they ghosted CMMI. They won because they focused their efforts in pre-acquisition, built relationships, and collected intelligence.

CMMI was one small but powerful piece.

That is ghosting. That is influencing the acquisition.

#4. GSA Schedule

When it comes to opportunities released on GSA Schedule, you don't often get the same 'blow-back' from industry when opportunities are released on other contract vehicles; such as ITES, NETCENTS, OASIS, SeaPort-e, and countless other agency and government wide contract vehicles.

While many opportunities for GSA Schedule are available on SAM, quite a few are not. Without a GSA Schedule, you do not have access to GSA e-Buy, the bidding portal for schedule holders. Out of sight is out of mind.

So, if you do not have a GSA Schedule, odds are you do not know what you are missing anyway. In general, only around 10% of procurements are on GSA Schedule. The percentages for every industry are different.

Then the following situation unfolds. Your company engages targets of opportunity throughout the first half of the year. Any opportunity on SAM that looks good, you engage. But if you have attended one of my training events or listened to the Podcast Game Changers for Government Contractors, *you know that you need three annual targets.*

As an example, you research the Federal Procurement Data System (fpds.gov) NOTE [10] or USASpending.gov and identify the following three targets for buying what you sell:

- The Food and Drug Administration (FDA) under Health and Human Services (HHS)

- The Department of the Interior (DOI), and

- Army Material Command (AMC)

These are the three agencies and military commands that you have decided to focus on this year. You have been building relationships, collecting intelligence, and working with your teaming partners.

During pre-acquisition (focus on the agency versus a specific opportunity) you learn from the Department of the Interior (DOI) that a sources-sought will be released to identify if there are small businesses interested in a fairly large technology project.

One of the questions on the sources-sought is to identify if you have a GSA Schedule, your GSA Schedule number, and to provide two past-performances.

Often times, without regard to industry preference, the government has already made a tentative decision to use or not use the GSA Schedule as part of the acquisition strategy.

If you have a GSA Schedule, that is awesome! But a sources-sought is a pre-acquisition tool. Anything can change! If the final acquisition strategy uses GSA Schedule and you have a Schedule, you have just barred-entry to thousands of small businesses that do not have a GSA Schedule.

But what are you going to do to ensure the government does not change the strategy?

If you do not have a GSA Schedule, what can you do and how do you do it?

Both situations can be ghosted!

If you have a GSA Schedule, here is one ghosting example:

---

[10] FPDS is migrating into the Integrated Award Environment (IAE) and will be part of System for Award Management (SAM) in 2020.

We would recommend that you implement this acquisition through GSA Schedule Category X with special item number Y. Our Schedule is GS-10F-0186I. With more than 500 vendors, with proven track records, releasing via schedule will simplify the acquisition and guarantee government negotiated rates. NOTE [11]

There is no right or wrong way to ghost a recommendation to use or confirm use of a GSA Schedule. I provided just one example above. If your company has a GSA Schedule but have never won a contract with it (which is more than half of all companies with a GSA Schedule), there are no limits to supporting statements that you can ghost. For example:

Additionally, this would be our first contract with the Department of the Interior. While we have past performance with Coca Cola, Mid-Town Bank, and the National Park Service, we are planning to bid 5% below our GSA Schedule rates. Based on our past performance and heavily discounting our GSA rates, we plan on competitively responding to the solicitation.

Let's look at this recommendation. Not only did I ghost a recommendation to use GSA Schedule, but I also ghosted proof of past performance. Yes, you always have a section for past performance, but I also want to ghost proof of performance in one or more of the ghosted recommendations!

And then I ghosted a 5% discount. I used the phrase "heavily discounting" but that is subjective. It may or may not be heavy. What I am really saying is, "If the government releases this opportunity on GSA Schedule, we are going to give the government great pricing."

Remember – if you want to influence the acquisition, you want to start looking at sources-sought as an opportunity to get inside the government's decision cycle. Similar to acquisition codes, do not simply look at it and say,

---

[11] The General Services Administration (GSA) manages a program called the Federal Marketplace Strategy. This program office is managing the consolidated schedule solicitation that is merging all 24 multiple awards schedules (GSA Schedules) into single schedule. This process is already underway and will use large categories, sub categories, and special item numbers. The roll out of the consolidated schedule program will likely be complete by end of calendar year 2020. For more information, visit https://www.gsa.gov/about-us/organization/federal-acquisition-service/fas-initiatives/federal-marketplace-strategy

"Yep. I have that." If you want the government to maintain an acquisition method, then ghost to reinforce so the government does not change it!

Now, if you are reading this and you do not have a GSA Schedule, you are thinking, "Fine, Josh, but if companies with GSA Schedules use this strategy, what can I possibly do to keep the government from using a GSA Schedule?

The answer is that you have to ghost a recommendation that creates a perception that it is not in the government's best interests to use a schedule. Here is one example:

"We recommend that the acquisition be a small business set-aside, released open-market in order to obtain industry leadership from companies with large corporation and government past performance. While there are several hundred small businesses on GSA Schedule that can support this requirement, the industry has made a major shift in the last 15 months and industry best-practices have shifted.

This acquisition for the Department of the Interior (DOI) is potentially a foundation for future requirements and projects. Based on our experience and past performance, we recognize that DOI will have future integration points for follow-on projects. Based on shifts in industry best-practices, specifically to cloud-based integrations, the government is likely to increase their spend on subsequent projects if these new baselines are not anticipated and planned for. Specifically, in terms of migrations from legacy systems to cloud-based deployments, three best-practices have shifted. They include. . ."

You never lie. You never ghost an inaccurate or untruthful recommendation. But in today's digital age, whether you provide technology, construction services, environmental, staffing, or you sell office supplies, there are always changes in your industry. As a professional, you should know the current status of your industry and the changes taking place.

Simply use one or more of those changes or trends to imply that this is one of those situations where releasing on Schedule may not be in the government's best interest. Releasing on GSA Schedule is not a bad option, but full and open is not a bad option either.

There are other ways to ghost having or not having a GSA Schedule.

* * *

I have just provided four different examples of ghosting. It is an amazingly important part of your sales tool-kit.

It takes practice.

You need to think differently about how you approach your relationships, how you respond to a sources-sought, the value of focusing your activities in pre-acquisition, how to communicate competitive advantage, and barring-entry to your competition.

Based on the products you sell or the services you provide, what can you ghost and how can *you* influence acquisitions?

Something to think about.

Chapter 5.
Redefining Your Capability Statement

This lesson is going to remind you that the basics are more important than ever. Let's talk about your capability statement. If you are new to government sales, a capability statement is simply a one or two-page marketing brochure.

I know… everyone has an opinion. Do this. Do that. There will never be a shortage of folks that will tell you how to update your capability statement. There are consultants that will review your capability statement at no cost. It's a brilliant B2B marketing strategy. Once they review, they explain why you need to work with them. My company doesn't do this. We have other products, services, and platforms that provide a pipeline funnel of opportunities for the company. But I would be less than honest if I did not admit that these companies have a brilliant marketing concept. Nothing wrong with it and it works. But I digress.

Okay, back to basics. Let's make sure you understand when to use a capability statement and a couple of pitfalls and recommendations.

First, you only get six seconds.

That is the average amount of time someone will look at your capability statement. Whether it is a government prospect, a small business counselor, or a prospective teaming partner, *you get six seconds*. Six seconds to communicate corporate maturity, capability, and value. You will be hard-pressed to find anyone that has reviewed your entire capability statement.

Second, 99% of printed copies go in the trash. Many small businesses are told to take a copy with them to one-on-one meetings. Unless you are told to bring it with you, I recommend against this. Simply email it when you get back to your office. Providing paper-copies, as a general rule, prevents you from properly positioning with that prospect after the meeting. I will discuss this in more detail in a moment.

Third, do not pay a company to develop your capability statement for you. PTACs and consultants can provide templates, but *you* are the one most likely to understand the value, as perceived by your clients, for your products and services. My company, RSM Federal, will help clients review and update their capability statement. But that is after we have spent several hours discussing strategy and 'Competency-Mapping™' their capabilities and past performance. Simply looking at a company's website is not enough to create a powerful capability statement. NOTE [12]

If you are like most companies, you already have a capability statement. If you're new to the market and don't have one, you can download two templates at https://rsmfederal.com/insider. You can only access the free Power Pack if you bought this book.

You should always tweak and update your capability statement. In fact, you should update it *every single time* you send it to a government prospect or a potential teaming partner. You should update it every time you have a new contract. You should update it every time the company or key personnel acquire new certifications.

But before you tweak it again, let's go back to basics and discuss the foundation of your capability statement.

Your capability statement is not simply a list of the products you sell or the services you provide.

Why should I care about what you sell? There are a hundred companies that sell what you sell. It does not matter that you are minority-owned, woman-owned, or veteran-owned. There are a hundred companies that sell what you sell with the exact same small business statuses. And this is exactly the risk you need to mitigate in your capability statement (and on your website). This is also the reason why your small business status can be detrimental if you don't understand how to position and take advantage of it.

---

[12] Competency-mapping is a step-by-step process for researching, documenting, and marketing the capabilities and past performance of a company and its employees. Designed by RSM Federal, the step-by-step process is available to RSM Federal clients as well as Members of the Federal Access Knowledge-Base.

If you have heard me speak at government conferences, you heard my mantra before. *"It is not what you sell. It is the value that your products and services provide."*

When you look at your capability statement, value is communicated in several locations. Your opening or introduction paragraph should have numbers and percentages. These are the metrics, the value that your products and services provide to your customers. It is not your opinion. It is not what you 'think' your customers are receiving in value. It is the value your customers *have achieved* using your products and services.

If your company is like most companies, you may be saying, "Well... I know we provide value but I have no detailed feedback, numbers, percentages, or other metrics from our customers." If this is the case, you need to call your past and current customers and perform Competency-Mapping™. When you first attempt to collect value metrics, most of your customers will say, "I don't know. You did a good job. It works," and nothing more. You have to steer the conversation and ask questions where the answers will provide you with the value you are looking for.

Value is also identified on your capability statement in your section on past performance. Past performance is just 'government-speak' for your experience, your past contracts.

The easiest way to communicate past performance is to list your corporate and government customers. Without a doubt, seeing a list of contracts is either the first or second item that everyone looks for on your capability statement. Seeing a list of clients gives the perception that you know what you are doing. I'm also looking to see if you have contracts with an agency or military command that I am targeting.

Let me go off on a tangent. If you have no corporate past performance, *then use your individual past performance*. This is common for new companies that do not have any sales or contracts. If you and two other business professionals started a company last week and each of you managed contracts for other companies, then use your combined individual performance. Instead of saying, "Big Wall Construction has worked with the Army, with Enterprise Rent-a-Car, or with the Department of Commerce," simply say, *"Our team* has worked with. . . or *our leadership* has worked with..."

Every capability statement has a section for your products and services. They are often labeled 'Capabilities.' I've lost count for the number of times

I have looked at a company's capability statement and asked myself, "exactly what do they do?" It looks like they are just listing a bunch of disparate capabilities in the hope of winning a contract.

Whether you are a one-woman company or a company with 100 employees, it is not what you *can* sell or the services you *can* provide. I am not saying you should not list new products or services you want to start selling. But what specifically is your company good at? The old adage still applies. Picking a specific service group or product category as your primary capability lets me know *that you have a focus,* that you have a niche, and you understand where you fall within your industry.

Another pitfall are companies that list project or program management as a core capability. This is one of the most common discussions that I have with clients. First, do not put project or program management on your capability statement unless that is pretty much all you do. For example, if your services include standing-up project management organizations (PMO) and consulting on PMOs for other organizations, then yes, include it.

Everyone that wins a contract, *as a prime,* is required to perform project or program management. If you are really good at project management and you are trying to get on a team as a subcontractor, you are *highly unlikely* to get a project management position. Why? Several reasons. First, no prime is going to give-up a management position on the contract that they can fill themselves. Most positions that are identified "key personnel" by the government in the RFP are also unlikely to be subcontracted. I am not talking about all positions. There are no absolutes. But if it is a management position that has direct interaction with the client, the prime is most likely to fill that position.

How do most companies increase their revenue by 50% in any given year? They win contracts with past and existing clients. If I am the prime, I am not likely to give a subcontractor a position that directly interacts with the government client. I want my company to position for whatever future projects are coming down the road. The way I do this is by maintaining ownership of communications with the client. This is how I protect the information and intelligence I collect.

So that you understand how all these pieces come together, let me take this one step further. Have you ever signed a teaming agreement (TA) with another company? If you have not, then you are likely new to government sales. After only a few months of talking with other companies, you will likely receive a teaming agreement from a prime contractor. After you have signed a dozen teaming agreements for a dozen teaming opportunities, (or you have primed and created your own teaming agreements), you will realize that almost all teaming agreements have common sections and language.

One of these sections discusses what you can and cannot do as a subcontractor. One common section says,

"The subcontractor is not authorized to communicate with the government without first talking to the Prime. In the event the government contacts the subcontractor, the subcontractor has 24 hours to notify the prime of the conversation and purpose of the discussion."

Now you have a better understanding why prime contractors almost always assume the project or program management role. The prime is using that role to generate new business. The prime is using the teaming agreement to prevent subcontractors from communicating directly with the client.

Also, listing project management, as a core capability on your capability statement, screams 'small business.' It implies that you do not understand the role of project management on federal procurements.

There are always exceptions when it comes to listing project management on your capability statement. Hopefully you will consider the points I have made. This does not mean you can't have a section on project and program management on your website. You can make it clear that you have exceptional and best-in-class project managers. Just weave it into the narrative of your various website sections.

Most service contracts require project management. It is industry and market agnostic. Since every company has to provide project management, regardless of the service, does that not imply that every company must have project management as a capability? Unless your company primarily supports PMO type contracts, focus on your other capabilities. It is assumed, and validated through your past performance and management narrative in the proposal, that you can successfully manage a project. If you still feel a need to list project management in your capability statement, put it at the bottom of your list.

The easiest way to break down your product or service offerings is to create two to four primary categories and list-out the solutions you sell, or want to sell, within those categories.

Next, you need to list your clients. I will argue that this is the most important part of your capability statement. No, your socio-economic status is *NOT* the most important and no, you should NOT have small business, 8a, woman-owned, Veteran, Service-Disabled, or HUBZone at the top of your capability statement! Are you a company that is woman-owned or a company that provides value? Yes, I am beating a dead horse, but this will be a common point throughout the book.

If you have a dozen or more contracts, even if you are a subcontractor on every one, you want to list them. Use categories, such as DoD, Federal, State and Local, Commercial, etc. If you have worked with four school districts and three different clients for solar power – then you may want to consider categories for education and energy.

It is common sense when you think of your past performance this way.

If you only have three or four contracts, whether you are the prime or subcontractor, I would list these *using logos versus text*. For example, let's say you have been a prime or subcontractor on an Army contract, an Air Force contract, a FEMA contract, and a Customs and Border Protection (CBP) contract.

That is four agency or Department of Defense (DoD) logos. That's Army, Air Force, FEMA, and CBP. *But I would also use the logos for DoD and for Homeland Security.*

That's a total of six logos. Army and AF fall under DoD and FEMA and CBP fall under DHS. It's marketing.

Remember, *you have six seconds to communicate corporate maturity and value.* Six versus four logos does not seem that big of a deal... but when you have six seconds, six versus four facilitates a greater perception of maturity. *You want every perceptual advantage you can get.*

Some professionals will tell you that it is against regulation to use federal and military logos / seals without approval of that organization's public affairs office (PAO). They are absolutely correct. Those are the regulations. However, in my 30 years in the government market, I have *never* seen a company get in trouble for it.

A picture is worth a thousand words. *You have six seconds.*

If you are new to government sales and need help developing a capability statement, go to your local PTAC and they will help you for free. If you have been in the market for a couple years and you want some real-world examples, with templates that you can modify yourself, you can download a capability statement template pack at www.rsmfederal.com/product-catalog.

Just remember, if you cannot communicate the value of your products and services, then you will have a hard time creating a capability statement and winning contracts.

So what makes a 'powerful' capability statement? There aren't any. There's a lot of marketing about how to create a powerful capability statement. It's just marketing. The government is unlikely to buy from you because they saw your capability statement. Teaming partners are unlikely to team with you simply because they saw your capability statement. Is it an important tool for small businesses? Absolutely. But the most it will do is open doors. You still have to step through and prove your value. In some situations, if your capability statement provides no value, then you are never walking through the door.

Communicating value is not the specifications of your product. It is not the type of services you sell. It is the quantifiable and qualifiable value that your customers get from your products and services. If you are struggling with 'value', it is likely impacting your capability statement, your website, your sales pitch, and how you introduce yourself at meetings, events, and conferences. It truly is the foundation for how you position in the market.

Before you update your capability statement again, put it down, stare at your wall, and imagine you are talking to me.

Tell me what you do and the value of the products or services you provide.

I want to hear numbers and percentages.

I want to hear adjectives, adverbs, and statements that communicate value.

Once you can do that - *then* update your capability statement. After that, update your website. After that, update your elevator pitch.

Think like a business professional. Know your value before you start marketing. A capability statement is nothing more than a one-page marketing brochure.

Every now and then you have to go back to basics.

Something to think about.

Chapter 6.
Do Not Take Your Capability Statement To Prospect Meetings

Continuing our strategies on capability statements, for most meetings, I recommend that you *not* take copies of your capability statement to meetings with the government or with teaming partners.

But what do I do when they ask for one in my meeting? Simply say you will email a copy when you get back to the office. Easy.

Yes, this goes against what is recommended by many consultants, and small business specialists. If you simply hand them your capability statement, are you positioning for competitive advantage?

No.

The only thing you have accomplished is providing your government prospect or prospective teaming partner with *generic* marketing collateral.

As an example, let's assume you are a technology company. You provide five core services. Your company provides database administration, application development, mobile applications, network engineering, and data analytics. Your capability statement lists these services, in this order, down the right side of your capability statement. In the introduction paragraph, where you introduce your company, you identify your company as a software engineering firm.

You have a meeting with a program manager at the Internal Revenue Service (IRS) that manages several large technology programs. After 45 minutes, you leave his office having collected information and intelligence on current and future contract opportunities. The two requirements that came-up over and over again were database administration and data analytics. You have database administration as your number one capability on your capability statement. That's great! But data analytics is at the bottom of your list of capabilities. Furthermore, your introduction paragraph mentions nothing about database administration or analytics.

This takes five minutes! Reorder your capabilities so that the two core services or solutions the program manager is looking for are at the top of your capability list! Rewrite your introduction paragraph to communicate that you specialize in those two capabilities.

Do not hand out copies during your meetings.

Tailor after each meeting and then send via email.

It makes sense! It's smart business. It allows you to position and gives you a reason to follow-up after your meeting.

Something to think about.

Chapter 7.
Category Management

I f you are unfamiliar with Category Management, it will likely become one of the most important pieces of your overall market and sales strategy. I've written several articles on LinkedIn and presented training seminars on how to approach category management. Due to the speed in which category management has taken over federal acquisition, I added this chapter for the second edition.

This chapter includes background on strategic sourcing and category management. It is designed to help you first understand the underlying principles so that you will better understand my recommendations

There are several critical chapters in this book. I often start these chapters with a note on their importance to your business. The concepts in this chapter are so important that if you fail to take them into account, your company will likely fail in government sales.

Let me take this a step further. If your company has successfully operated in the government market, whether five or twenty years, if you fail to take these concepts into account, you will more than likely lose your current market share.

Category Management is the future of government acquisition.

Background

Almost every acquisition strategy and model used by the government is some form of strategic sourcing and category management.

There is often confusion between Strategic Sourcing and Category Management. I've sometimes used the two interchangeably but they truly are two distinct and separate strategies.

Strategic sourcing is a procurement process where an organization (in this case the government) continually reviews its procurement needs. If done correctly, it helps the organization better forecast and *define pricing*.

Category Management is a structured and strategic approach for procuring products and services. Unlike strategic sourcing that focuses on pricing, category management focuses on *specific areas of spend*. Goods and services are broken down into specific groups and related categories. Each category is then managed by a specific individual or business unit.

While strategic sourcing and category management are separate strategies, when combined, they operate in tandem and provide extensive value.

The most widely recognized (and discussed) government strategic sourcing program is the General Services Administration's (GSA) Federal Strategic Sourcing Initiative (FSSI). While still in use, it experienced both setbacks and extensive backlash from industry. To be fair, every new program has setbacks.

The government put a great spin on the value of FSSI. But this program turned industry upside down. For example, if your company was not selected to be on the office supply FSSI contract - it was highly difficult, if not impossible, to sell office supplies *in volume*.

Back in August 2016, I sat down with Congressman Luetkemeyer and Senator McCaskill's staff – representing the House of Representatives and the US Senate, Republican and Democrat. I walked through the numbers of what happened to small businesses when office supplies fell under strategic sourcing via the FSSI program.

The government said it was an acquisition like any other and that they were taking advantage of strategic sourcing principles. However, Congress and the community at large were not told that the manager GSA hired to roll-out the FSSI program had just tested it on the state level.

Back in 2003, the Deputy Secretary for Administration and Procurement for the Pennsylvania Department of General Services, developed and implemented a state-wide strategic sourcing initiative. It was this program that laid the foundation for GSA's FSSI program.

Several points. First, in 2008, the state of Pennsylvania performed an audit of their strategic sourcing program. As a result of this audit, the program was downgraded and eventually terminated. [13]

Prior to the program being terminated, the Pennsylvania Deputy Secretary for Administration and Procurement was hired by the General Services Administration (GSA) to develop a strategic sourcing program for the U.S. Government. This was the genesis for GSA's FSSI program.

When GSA awarded the FSSI contracts, they told government buyers to *only purchase office supplies from FSSI vendors.* This meant that companies who had been selling to the government for years, who did not make it onto FSSI, were no longer authorized to sell their goods to the government (except for micro-purchases). This included hundreds of companies whose primarily revenue was government sales.

While GSA Schedule holders are but one small subset of the overall contractor community, approximately 90% of the small business GSA Schedule 75 holders *were instantly cut off from selling to the government.*

Hundreds of small office supply companies went out of business overnight.

What is Category Management?

At its core, category management is *leveraging purchasing power.* By its very nature and how it is able to provide value, it requires that *less vendors supply a given product or service.* It means the government can be heavy-handed and say, *"If you want to be on this contract, you'll be one of very few vendors who will have guaranteed revenue,* **but you have to lower your pricing**."

What they're not saying but is clearly the case - *you must lower your margins.* From a business perspective, this makes perfect sense.

Yes, there's a tradeoff. If you lower your margins but greatly increase your sales volume, you are going to make more money overall, *albeit at*

---

[13] Federal Acquisition Regulation on Strategic Sourcing – Comment to FAR Case 2015-015, Strategic Sourcing and Category Management Programs Impacting the United States Small Business Community; Joshua Frank, September 6, 2015.

lower margins. As a government contractor, if you fail to get on the contract, you're pretty much shut-out of the market.

Let me go off on another tangent. As a tax payer, strategic sourcing and category management are critical to future cost control and for a better streamlined acquisition process. On the other hand, strategic sourcing and category management does not **automatically** take into account the full impact to the business community; or *attempt to achieve the necessary balance required by both sides of the supply chain.*

Category Management Examples

Listing all the examples that come to mind would take more than this chapter. There are now hundreds of examples in federal acquisition. So here are several major category management initiatives that are taking place that you may not have even realized fell under category management.

- Multiple Award Task Order Contracts (MATOCs) and Indefinite Delivery Indefinite Quantity Contracts (IDIQs). When you've been in the market for a number of months, you'll recognize these acquisition mechanisms. They are methods of category management; less contractors at highly competed prices.

- Blanket Purchase Agreements (BPAs). Like GSA Schedules, MATOCs, and IDIQs, they've been around forever. BPAs are a method for category management.

- GSA Consolidated Schedule. In late 2019, GSA moved all 24 GSA Schedules into a single consolidated schedule with categories and subcategories. The most widely recognized and popular government contract mechanism has been modified to support the principles and gain value from category management.

- The Defense Logistics Agency's (DLA) Internet Bid Board System (DIBBS) alerted industry in late 2019 that DLA had started issuing automated Indefinite Delivery Contracts (AIDC) below Simplified Acquisition Thresholds ($250,000). AIDCs are defined as long-term contracts for a single material that DLA stocks and generally plans to order multiple times per year. The coverage period is one year. These contracts will have a guaranteed contract minimum quantity. This is another case where a company could be selling consistently throughout the year, fail to get on the AIDC, and be locked-out of the market for a year.

- If you sell medical supplies, textiles, or other product used by military and VA hospitals, your products must be on what is called the 'Formulary.' If your products are not on the formulary, you're not selling your products. The formulary has been around for years but it is a clear form of category management.

- Have you heard of the Medical Surge Prime Vendor (MSPV) Program? There are two; one for the Department of Veterans Affairs (VA) and one for the Department of Defense (DoD). If you're not one of the Prime Vendors, all you can be is a supplier. Competition to be a supplier is intense. Most Prime Vendors have their preferred suppliers. It's no surprise that many medical contractors were screaming about lack of sales at a recent Department of Veterans Affairs conference.

Recommendations

At this point, you understand that strategic sourcing and category management work hand-in-hand and that it is the future of government procurement.

As Category Management expands across the government, *the industry-base will contract.* By its very nature, the more category management takes hold, the fewer government contractors. That's how it works. Whether we are talking about the government or a Fortune 500 company, it's about leveraging an organization's purchasing power. By default, this also implies and requires that contractors and vendors compete and drive pricing down.

Category Management is the future of government acquisition.

If you don't plan for category management in your sales strategy, you'll wake up one morning and not understand how you lost market share. I saw this happen five times last year to five different companies. They failed to pay attention to what was happening in the government market.

Now, the sky is not falling. Companies that follow my recommendations below will not only be fine, they'll be successful. I mentioned in Chapter 2 that 50% of companies with a GSA Schedule fail to successfully win government contracts (at least $25,000 annually). Why do half of GSA Schedule holders fail? Because they don't understand how to use their GSA Schedule.

The same goes for preparing your company for category management. If you plan for it now, you'll be fine. But you have to plan for it in your business and sales strategies.

Here are my recommendations.

Recommendation #1 - Situational Awareness

No matter what you sell, you need to be aware of how the government currently buys your products or services AND how your prospects and clients are planning to change their acquisition strategies.

We're talking about information and intelligence. The term 'situational awareness' is a military term. It refers to understanding everything that is happening around you and happening to you.

Let's assume for a moment that your company sells office supplies. It's the year prior to GSA releasing the FSSI procurement. Your company is consistently making $7.5 million every year from clients with the Department of Defense (DoD), the Department of Labor (DOL), and the Department of Homeland Security (DHS). Sure, you have a ton of credit card buys, but the vast majority of your revenue comes from large buys over the simplified acquisition threshold ($250,000).

You had no idea that GSA was going to include office supplies under FSSI or even that FSSI existed.

Yes, hundreds of companies went out of business but why didn't they know that they were about to lose their entire market share?

The answer is that they focused solely on current sales and not their customers internal discussions for the future. Most of these companies were simply taking orders and making money. They were not asking questions and collecting information and intelligence from their customers on the future of their command's or agency's procurement plans.

Just last year, a company reached out to me. They were slowly losing market share to the tune of $1 million a year. Every year one of the products in their product line would be given to a single company or group of companies under an IDIQ or similar contract vehicle. It never dawned on them that what they were seeing was a mass move, albeit by individual product, towards category management. Even though they recognized that category management was taking over their market, instead of seeking information and intelligence, they simply pushed their sale's team harder to make-up for the lost sales.

As you can imagine, they did not make-up the losses. Today, they have one senior business developer who is responsible for maintaining situational awareness so the next time one of their products is being moved under category management, they'll know six to twelve months before it happens. This will allow the company to build the necessary relationships, collect the necessary intelligence to be competitive, and influence the solicitation!

So the first recommendation is to gain situational awareness for all your prospects and current clients. This means asking them questions on how they will be acquiring your products or services in the future.

For example, *"Hi Janet, thanks for the contract but I have a question for you. We've been selling to you for years. We're always putting small buys on the purchase card (credit card) and larger buys via GSA Schedule. By any chance has there been discussion, either in your office or the agency as a whole, on the topic of strategic sourcing or category management? Has there been discussion about consolidation of contracts, grouping of products or services, or changes to how you'll be buying our products and services in the future?"*

Build situational awareness into your overall government strategy. When you build it in, you have the information and intelligence you need. You'll ensure that you don't get surprised when the government releases a solicitation under category management that covers your products or services.

Situational awareness will also ensure that you're more competitive when the time comes.

Recommendation #2 – Engage 2-3 MATOCs / IDIQs Every Year

Getting onto a Multiple Award Task Order Contract (MATOC), a Multiple Award Contract (MAC), an Indefinite Delivery Indefinite Quantity (IDIQ) Contract, or any other umbrella contract vehicle is more important today than ever before.

All companies that sell to the government today are aware of the difference between single contracts and multiple award contracts. Single contracts go to a single contractor. Multiple award contracts are awarded to multiple companies that must (normally) then compete on future task orders.

Even if you didn't understand category management before reading this chapter, think about it for a minute. If an organization wants to streamline their procurements and drive down prices, how would you do it? You would have *all your current vendors compete against each other*, competitively drive down each other's pricing to be competitive, and then select only a small number to ensure that you're obtaining the *best pricing based on volume*.

This is exactly what MATOCs, MACs, and IDIQs do. They are a form of category management.

Knowing this, your company cannot operate as it has in the past. If you've been primarily focused on single award contracts, you need to immediately shift some of your strategy to MATOCs, MACs, and IDIQs. If you have a GSA Schedule, that alone is not enough! There were several hundred companies with a GSA Schedule that failed to get on the office supply FSSI contract and their sales dried-up overnight.

For many readers, you're thinking, "Yes, I understand the power of multiple award contracts, but they're so hard to win."

Yes, they are. They are highly competitive.

You need to recognize that without being a prime or subcontractor on these contract vehicles, you're going to see your sales drop. It won't happen overnight but it'll likely happen over the next couple years. (There are no absolutes in business and some companies, based on what they sell, especially niche products or services, will be less impacted. However, most products and services can achieve the leverage and value of category management.)

So, recommendation number two is to ensure that your company is engaging two to three major MATOCs, MACs, and IDIQs *every year*. The only way to successfully engage two to three every year is to engage them in pre-acquisition and to collect information and intelligence from your buyers.

If your business is purely transactional without strong conversations with your prospects and clients, you're going to be in trouble in the years ahead.

Recommendation #3 - Multi-Pronged Bidding Approach

For every large MATOC, MAC, or IDIQ, you want to engage with multiple bids. Now that you understand the importance of category management and how it impacts the market, you need to maximize your chances for getting on these vehicles.

For example, even though you can bid as prime and believe you have an excellent chance of being one of the winning bids, you also need to be a subcontractor on one or more other teams. You'll likely bump into exclusivity clauses so you'll likely be able to only subcontract on one team. But you need to maximize your strategy.

Most companies think, "We're not going to be a subcontractor on one of our competitor's teams! We want to win it and being a subcontractor is like admitting defeat or admitting we can't win it."

No, it's not. If your proposal is the best, you are going to win. If your proposal is the best but your pricing is 5% higher, you'll probably lose. Making a mistake on your Competitive Price Point (CPP), discussed in Chapter 14, will likely sink your bid. So having other win options is always a smart strategy!

If you're thinking, "Our competitor won't put us on their team! What possible reason could we give them for doing that?"

The answer is that you *have information and intelligence that will make the overall team more competitive. You've been engaging the customer pre-acquisition!*

To summarize, you need to engage two to three multiple award contract opportunities every year. That's a minimum.

There's no right answer to this. Every company is different. But I would consider using a metric of 10%. 10% of all the opportunities in your pipeline should be multiple award contract opportunities. This is how you ensure that your business and sales strategy is taking category management into account.

Your Next Steps

Whether you are new to government sales or been in the market for decades, you need to build category management into your business and sales strategy. For companies that are new to the market, you are not far behind the curve. Most experienced companies are simply not paying attention to category management.

You need to collect information and intelligence from your prospects and current buyers. You need to strengthen your situational awareness.

You need to engage multiple opportunities every year for MATOCs, MACs, and IDIQs. Without fail.

You need to maximize your strategy with a multi-pronged bidding approach. Whenever possible, don't simply attempt to prime, also try to get on several teams. Yes, it is more effort… but that's smart business strategy.

How does your current business and sales strategy take category management into account?

If you're in government sales, *it must be taken into account*.

Something to think about.

Chapter 8.
What Are Your Three Annual Targets?

I am going to touch on a common challenge companies have in government sales. We are going to talk about targeting the overall government market versus your annual target list. You cannot simply 'look' for opportunities that meet your NAICS codes. Well, you can, but you are unlikely to win many contracts.

You need to systematically target a select number of agencies in order to build relationships and collect intelligence.

Every company should identify who buys what they sell, how much they buy, and how often they buy it. This is researched in order to identify your target market for both federal agencies and military commands. Identifying who buys what you sell, how much they buy, and how often they buy is what I call 'propensity.'

Propensity
Identifying who buys what you sell, how much they buy,
and how often they buy it.

As part of your company's sales strategy you should identify three or four federal agencies or military commands that consistently buy what you sell. These three agencies or military commands are your *annual targets*.

To identify propensity, you'll use either USASpending.gov or the Federal Procurement Data System (FPDS) (which is currently being migrated into the Integrated Award Environment (IAE) which includes the System for Award Management (SAM).

Your three annual targets should not simply be US Army or Department of Transportation (DOT). You want to identify two or three subordinate activities that you will specifically target within the Army or the Department of Transportation over the next twelve months. If you have a sales team (one or more business developers), *this is one means of measuring their focus.*

You research who buys what you sell, how much, and how often. The results might be the Department of Homeland Security (DHS), the US Army, and the Department of Commerce (DOC). Under each of these three targets you will have two or three subordinate targets. For example, in DHS you identify that the Federal Emergency Management Agency (FEMA) and US Customers and Border Protection (CBP) buy what you sell. In the Army, there are three major commands and the same with CBP. In total, you may have six or eight organizations that fall under your three annual targets.

But what about all those other great opportunities you find outside these targets? Do you only focus on those three agencies or commands? How much of your time should you spend on them?

When I coach companies and help develop a tailored sales strategy, this is always a topic of discussion, confusion, and angst. So, here is some simple guidance on how to approach the market. And if you are not already doing this, it will change how you approach government sales.

First, your sales strategy falls into two buckets: *acquisition and pre-acquisition.* If you learn about an opportunity before the RFP or RFQ is released in the System for Award Management (SAM), it is pre-acquisition. The exception are sources sought and draft solicitations. These are pre-acquisition. But in general, if the first time you hear about an opportunity is when you see the RFP on SAM, then it is already in acquisition.

Now, what about the three agencies you identified as your three annual targets? Your market strategy is to focus on pre-acquisition, before they release RFPs or RFQs! *You are not focused on specific opportunities. You are focused on building relationships. You are focused on collecting intelligence.* You are focused on learning about their organization and their challenges.

Your three annual targets are those agencies and commands that buy what you sell and *you engage them throughout the year*. You are identifying program managers, contracting officers, decision makers, going to industry days, attending conferences and small business events. Your primary focus for your annual targets is collecting intelligence and getting your name in front of them.

But what about opportunities on SAM that do not fall under your three annual targets?

You still qualify, engage, and bid.

Assuming your three annual targets are the Army, Homeland Security, and Department of Commerce, you see four opportunities on SAM for Interior, Energy and two for Air Force. None of these fall under your annual targets. Two are for sources sought, one is a draft solicitation, and the other is an RFP.

Obviously, your priority on these four are the two sources sought because you can influence the acquisition. They are pre-acquisition. But should you still qualify and possibly respond to the other two? There is no right answer! It depends on how competitive you will be.

Again, the focus for your three annual targets is to perform pre-acquisition activities.

You are engaging the market from both a strategic and tactical perspective. You are positioning in the market for strategic sales by engaging annual targets before RFPs are released. But as you are implementing strategic activities, you are engaging other qualified opportunities for tactical revenue and cash flow.

You are much more likely to win contracts for opportunities that fall within your targeted agencies and commands. Why? Because they know you! You have built a relationship with them. You have been collecting intelligence the last six months. You have acted strategically. You have intelligence that makes you more competitive than your competition.

Pre-Acquisition vs Acquisition.

Strategic vs Tactical.

Annual Target List = Pre-Acquisition Phase = Strategic

All Other Agencies / Opportunities = Acquisition Phase = Tactical

Which three agencies or military commands are your annual targets?

Something to think about.

Chapter 9.
Do You Have Enough Opportunities in Your Pipeline?

C ompanies that win contracts understand and practice the basics. Think about everything you have done over the last week. Go through your calendar and your emails and make a list of all the things you did.

Now, put a checkmark next to all the activities that you know will *directly influence* you winning a contract. Some of these include writing proposals, talking to teaming partners, and phone calls with government buyers and decision makers.

Then there are activities that are administrative, marketing, or what I call lost-thoughts. How often are you lost in thought, worried that what you're doing is not productive? How often are you putting out fires? How often are you dealing with employee issues? Yes, you have to deal with administrative issues, but how much time are you really spending on them?

You may be surprised at how little time you are actually spending on prospecting and sales. I am going to walk you through a strategy on how you can refocus your time and energy. You need to know how many opportunities (not contracts) you need in order to grow your company.

First, what is your revenue target? What is the company goal?

Let's assume your goal is $5 million.

Next, we need to identify your opportunity to sales ratio. Most small companies operate at 4:1 or 5:1. I prefer 5:1 because it mitigates risk. If you are new to government sales, I recommend 5:1. This means if you want to make $5 million, you need to have at least $25 million in your pipeline ($5 million at 5:1 ratio).

For many business professionals, when they first see their 5:1 number, they stress-out and say, "I have nowhere near that number today! There is no way I can do that this year." And this is not true. From a planning perspective, it does not mean you have to have $25 million in your pipeline today.

Let's assume it is October 1st, the first day of the government's fiscal year. Between now and August 1st, at least $25 million in opportunities need to be qualified and engaged. You want to have $25 million in qualified opportunities *over the next ten months*.

Don't forget, opportunities will be added and removed *every month*. Some you will decide are no longer qualified and others you may not have the resources to engage. Every month you will be adding new opportunities based on your bid-matching system, discussions with teaming partners, and from phone calls with government prospects.

You did notice that I said $25 million in qualified opportunities over the next 10 months? That would put us at August 1st. Why 10 months? Because that gives you 60 days to finalize and position for opportunities, not yet awarded, before the end of the fiscal year on September 30th.

Let's review. Step 1 is identifying your annual revenue target. Step 2 is identifying your opportunity to sale's ratio.

Step 3 is asking yourself, "for these $25 million in opportunities, what percentage should I *prime* and what percentage should I *subcontract*?

One of my most influential mentors, Dan Ragheb, once said to me, "Josh, it's not about the money. *It's about the money*."

Money is money. Whether you prime or subcontract, you are making money. Also remember that when you subcontract, the prime normally writes the proposal. That saves you a ton of time, money, and energy. It also **allows you to engage many more opportunities**.

More Bids With Existing Resources

A hybrid sales strategy is when you have both direct and indirect sales channels. Direct is prime. Indirect is subcontracting. One way to engage more opportunities with existing resources is to have other companies writing the

For many companies, especially in their first couple of years of selling to the government, I recommend the prime to subcontracting ratio be either 30 / 70 or 40 / 60. You are priming 40% of the opportunities and teaming as a subcontractor for 60%.

Initially, you will not see these percentages in your pipeline. But that is your goal. That is what you work towards over the first 10 months.

If you have twenty qualified opportunities in your pipeline, eight (8) are opportunities you plan to prime. You are going to bid / write proposals on these eight opportunities. But then you are going to subcontract to other companies on twelve (12) other opportunities. You are on various teams and most important, you do not have to write the proposals! This is why a strong teaming strategy will increase the *number of opportunities* in your pipeline by 400%! This is how companies successfully achieve their opportunity to sales ratio (especially smaller companies).

So, let's review. $5 million sales target requires $25 million in opportunities. Using twenty as an example, you are going to prime eight opportunities and subcontract on twelve. There are many other metrics you can use for breaking down the management of your pipeline. If you are minority or socially disadvantaged (8a), woman-owned, or veteran-owned, what percent of your opportunities are full and open versus set-aside for small business or for your status? Every company is different.

And then there is one final step. Step 4 is breaking down your opportunity to sales ratio by quarter. So, for a $5 million quota with a 5:1 ratio for $25 million, you need to have $6.25 million in opportunities by the end of the first quarter and every quarter thereafter.

This is very important! I see this time and again with our clients when we first start working with them. Many companies say, "Well, we need $25 million in opportunities" and then six months later they only have $3 million in their pipeline.

They should have $12.5 million.

It is difficult to catch-up. Make sure that once you identify your ratio that you set milestones each quarter to ensure you stay on track. This is critical not just for management, but for every sales professional or business developer on your staff.

If you don't do this, *you will not hit your revenue targets*. This is your baseline for success. Some companies say, "It only takes one contract!" That's not business strategy. That's praying.

Hope is not a strategy

With 60% subcontracting, it means you need to have a *strong teaming strategy*. There are a few companies, based on what they sell, that can focus primarily on a 100% priming strategy (no subcontracting). Most companies need a hybrid sales approach (priming and subcontracting) to maximize their opportunities in the government market.

By the way, indefinite delivery and indefinite quantity (IDIQ) contracts, government wide acquisition contracts (GWAC), and multiple award contracts (MAC), **do not count towards your opportunity to sale ratio** (In the current example, the $25 million). If you win an IDIQ, *only the task orders count towards your numbers*. This is a very important concept. Don't let yourself or your business developers add dollar amounts to these umbrella contracts.

Think about this for a minute. If you are going after a $10 million IDIQ, whether as prime or sub, you do not want to include that $10 million in your numbers. This is because even if you win and get on the IDIQ, *you do not make any money*. Umbrella type contracts do not get you any closer to your $5 million annual goal. You can only win a contract that generates revenue if you win a future task order on that umbrella contract.

Yes, you put IDIQs, GWACs, and MAC contracts on your pipeline, but *no revenue numbers*. Once you have won the contract, only give revenue numbers on task orders that fall under that contract.

You should engage a couple of IDIQs every year. This is especially important with the government's shift in strategic sourcing and category management. This is why I added a chapter on category management.

* * *

If you have not done this exercise, now is a perfect time to do it.

Once you have these numbers, think about how you are going to find these opportunities.

1) Have you completed your propensity research?

2) What are your three (3) annual strategic targets?

3) What is your annual revenue target?

4) What is your 5:1 opportunity to sales ratio?

5) How many qualified opportunities are required?

6) What are your prime / subcontract pipeline percentages?

7) How many government prospects do you need to call?

8) How many teaming partners do you need to have?

9) How many opportunities and at what value do you need by the end of the next quarter?

10) Now - *What percentage of your daily activities are actually helping you hit these numbers?*

It is about organization and prioritization.

Something to think about.

Chapter 10.
Walking Opportunities Through
Your Pipeline

I f you are not winning as many contracts as you would like, I want to help you look at business development in a more logical manner.

Winning contracts is about '**moving opportunities** *through* **your pipeline**.' This means you do not simply add unqualified opportunities to your pipeline and wait for the RFP or RFQ to drop. We are going to talk about business development, the challenges in winning government contracts, and the importance of moving opportunities through the pipeline and what that entails.

I have trained thousands of small business owners and sales professionals on government sales and there are several common challenges. In general, it is easy to get distracted by the simple tasks and a number of business developers either do not feel comfortable making calls or they procrastinate in favor of doing other activities.

There are three common challenges that many business developers face:

First, is "death by administration." You focus on spreadsheets, reviewing opportunities in your bid-matching system, and updating your customer relationship management (CRM) system (Zoho, Salesforce, etc.). Taking notes and updating spreadsheets feels like you are making progress when you are looking for reasons to not pick-up the phone.

Often times, a manager may ask for updates during weekly meetings. What do many business developers do? They focus on creating reports. Don't get me wrong, weekly sales updates are a necessary evil. How else will management know if sales professionals are meeting their objectives, hitting their numbers, or making the necessary number of calls? Reports are just that - reports. They are not a core sales activity.

The second challenge for business developers is an over-reliance on talking to teaming partners. For some owners, all they hear from a business developer is "I had a great conversation with this or that company. It was a great conversation and we are going to bid opportunities together."

A year later it dawns on the business developer, or the owner, that this teaming partner is no more mature than your company. This partner does not have the requisite past performance to be competitive or make you more competitive.

The third challenge is giving up. "They won't call me back. It always goes to voicemail. I have done everything I can. What can I do? They won't respond."

For the last one, bottom line, you either make it happen or you don't. It takes elbow grease, determination, and perseverance.

Many business developers give up. You must be *tenacious*.

These are the core challenges. Not only do business developers have to manage these challenges, *so does management.*

Some business owners are somewhat myopic and focus purely on the metrics. "Hey Mark, how many calls did you make? How many opportunities did you put in the pipeline this month? I sent you five SAM opportunities for bidding. When do they come out for bid?"

Every company needs to have sales metrics so that you know if what you are doing today will help achieve your revenue objectives tomorrow.

Whether you are the business developer or owner of the company, there is a practical exercise you can both perform to put your best foot forward and fix how you are executing business development.

If you are the business developer, you can do this without ever talking to your manager.

If you are the manager, you can influence your business developers and transform your sales strategy.

Start with metrics:

- How many new opportunities were identified in the last 30 days?

- How many RFPs are we expecting to see in the next two months?

- How many calls did you make this week to the government?

- How many calls did you make to teaming partners?

- What is our opportunity to sales ratio?

- What is our win rate? (Number of contracts won versus number of proposals or bids submitted)

- What percentage of our opportunities should be prime versus subcontracting?

- What percentage of our opportunities should be with agencies on our annual target list?

These are all important questions to help manage your sales strategy. *But even more important is how you move opportunities through your pipeline.*

To start, don't simply focus on the numbers. (Here we go again. I can hear some readers screaming at me. You JUST told us how important metrics are!)

Most opportunities enter your pipeline as *unqualified*. Yes, they want to buy what you sell but it may be the first time you became aware of that specific opportunity.

It does not matter if they are buying what you sell. When an opportunity first hits your pipeline, you do not know if you will be competitive. Simply selling what they are looking for is not enough. Is your pricing competitive? How many companies are likely to respond? Is there an incumbent?

If you identified the opportunity on SAM, GSA eBuy, or a bid-matching system, it is an unqualified opportunity (unless you knew it was coming out beforehand). **You need to qualify it**. Every opportunity moves through stages. Stages help you move the opportunity from unqualified, to qualified, to you becoming more and more competitive.

Most customer relationship management (CRM) tools and pipelines use stages. When you run a report in your CRM, you can quickly see how competitive you are on each opportunity. Most CRMs also allow you to tailor the stages. Why? Because the sale's cycle for product companies is different than service companies. Every company operates differently.

The stages are fairly standard. Every company will tailor and modify them based on what they sell and how they operate.

When it comes to opportunity stages on a pipeline, I use the following:

- Territory: In my territory but not yet qualified

- Qualified: have started to identify challenges we can resolve

- CO/KO: Spoke to the contracting officer

- DM: Spoke to a decision maker

- Shaping: I have started to shape the requirements through discussions with the prospect (or teaming partner)

- SS - Working: A sources sought was released and I am responding

- SS - No Response: No time to respond or missed it

- SS - Responded: I have responded to the sources sought

- RFP Released: RFP or RFQ has been released

- Proposal: In process of writing

- Source Selection: awaiting award

- WIN: We've won!

- Lose: We didn't win the contract

- Closed: Opportunity moved off pipeline for other reasons (Remember I told you that opportunities are constantly moving on and off your pipeline. You may have an unqualified opportunity that looks really good and then after talking to the decision maker, you choose to no-bid. This is a perfect example of an opportunity being 'Closed.'

Let's go off on another tangent. I like tangents. You are a business owner. Why would you want to track and run reports on the number of closed opportunities? Well, it can be quite informative. Imagine the following scenario. You have a business developer that hasn't been winning contracts but their activity looks awesome. Every week or month they are expertly walking you through all the new opportunities they've found. They show you how they are meeting the 5:1 opportunity to sales ratio and have done a wonderful job of hitting 40% prime to 60% subcontracting on listed opportunities.

But then you do something most wouldn't focus on. You review the number of opportunities closed over the last two months. Low and behold, you realize that opportunities are being closed and moved off the pipeline just as fast as new opportunities are being added.

This may or may not be a problem. But it could be a sign that the business developer is focused more on 'activity' and 'looking good' versus performing strong business development. Don't you want to catch this early versus waiting a year and trying to explain how you hit all your metrics but generated little revenue?

When I coach a sales team, there are two areas that I focus on. One is 'metrics' because that ensures your overall strategy is on track. The second is requiring business developers to walk me through how they are engaging each opportunity.

Example: "I found it on SAM and I checked the bid-matching tool. The contracting officer notes in the bid-matching tool say the RFP will release in three weeks." If that's it, then I know the company has no more than a 50 / 50 chance of winning the contract.

Instead, I ask the business developer to show me how they are *walking the opportunity through the pipeline.*

Where did you find this opportunity? SAM? Bid-match system? A conference? A teaming partner? The government called you?

Have you read the entire statement of work (SOW) and highlighted every direct and implied requirement? Can you provide 100% of what is required? If you can provide 100%, do you have the past performance to prime this effort? Will your past performance be strong enough to make you more competitive than other companies with similar past performance? If you can prime the effort, *should you*? Just because you can do 100% of the work, based on each direct and implied requirement, will your past performance be enough to make you competitive?

Oh, you are competitive? Why? Explain why you will be more competitive than the competition. Outline how your corporate background, the value of your products, services, and past performance are going to make you competitive.

If you plan to prime but you are only somewhat competitive, even if you can do 100% of the work, should you build a team to strengthen your offering? Which companies would you recommend for subcontractors? Why do you recommend them and what value do they bring and how do they make you more competitive?

Oh, you will not be competitive if you prime? Okay, which companies should you engage so you are a subcontractor on another team? You think you should be on McCarthy's team? Why are they more competitive than the other primes? What makes you think they have a competitive advantage? How will you make McCarthy's team *more competitive*?

Was there a sources sought? Did you respond to it or did you miss it? Have you reached out to the contracting officer? To the government program manager? If you cannot get them to respond, have you reached out to the small business office and asked for them to facilitate?

So you're building a team? Remember that one company at the conference two months ago? They have two contracts with this agency. Have you reached out to them to see if they are pursuing this opportunity?

Are you going to team with them even though you are not sure if they will be any more competitive than another teaming partner?

At the same time you are asking these questions, you are also focused on collecting intelligence. Although you have worked hard to collect intelligence that is not in the public domain (not on SAM or your bid-matching tool), you still do not have any groundbreaking updates.

Perhaps it is a sources-sought (pre-acquisition) with the Army Corps of Engineers (USACE). Are you going to attend the Society of American Military Engineer's (SAME) JETC Conference this spring to track down decision makers and ask questions? Or is it a contract with the Department of Veterans Affairs for Q2 next year. Are you going to attend the VA's National Veterans Small Business Engagement (NVSBE) conference or the National Veteran Small Business Coalition's (NVSBC) Veteran Entrepreneur Training Symposium (VETS) to track down folks running this contract and ask questions?

Do any of the opportunities on your pipeline have incumbents?

Are they eligible to recompete their contract?

Has the government had any issues with the incumbent contractor?

What percentage of the opportunities in your pipeline are new contracts versus recompetes?

For each of these opportunities, when did you last engage each one (I want to see dates) and what activities did you perform to get more information and to ensure you are making your company more and more competitive?

* * *

These are the type of questions that must be asked. Also consider that if the RFP was released yesterday, you should be able to think through these questions and have answers by the following day! These are the types of questions the top 1% of business developers will ask themselves.

Wow. I've just listed thirty odd questions that should be asked about each opportunity in the pipeline. Failure to think this way is why companies fail to consistently win contracts.

It's that simple and it's that complex.

It takes practice.

Have you ever heard of a process called the "bid - no bid" process? It is how you decide which opportunities in your pipeline you decide to pursue and respond to. If you don't have a bid – no bid process, you may want to read this chapter again. Grab a highlighter and highlight the various questions. If you need a one-page automated template for your bid - no bid, which is super helpful, I recommend the bid – no bid template that you can download in the Federal Access Knowledge-Base https://rsmfederal.com/FA

The Most Important Metric
Number of Monthly Responses

Based on what we've discussed so far, I also recommend that one of your company metrics be submitting two or three responses every month. This is a CORE metric the business owner must enforce.

If you don't bid, you don't win. All of the metrics we've discussed so far mean nothing if you aren't responding to sources sought and submitting bids and proposals.

They can be proposals for various opportunities where you are a subcontractor. They can be proposals that you are priming. They can be responses to a sources sought. *They can be any combination.*

It's the end of the month, how many responses have gone in? None? Then how are you going to make these up next month or by end of quarter?

If you don't bid, you don't win. One of the absolute most important metrics to meet is the number of responses your sales strategy requires every month and quarter.

Now think about the 30 questions that we walked-through earlier. Yes, you might ask some or many of these questions, but it is an informal exercise? Have you heard the phrase, "hope is not a strategy?" Mine is "Your gut is not a strategy." Having twenty opportunities in your pipeline and waiting for RFPs to drop is nothing more than copying information from SAM or a bid-matching system and waiting to respond.

Business Developers that do this do not win contracts.

You need to move opportunities *through your pipeline.* You need to move each opportunity through your sales funnel.

Each opportunity starts as being in your assigned territory. Then it moves to you collecting intelligence through phone calls and meetings. These could be with the government, partners, or both. Then it moves to you actually talking to a decision maker or influencer who has a vested interest in the outcome of the contract. (Yes, sometimes this is difficult or impossible to achieve. But you must make multiple attempts!) If there is a sources sought, you respond to it.

Regardless of there being a sources sought, you have started to influence the acquisition and ghost your strengths. Then it moves to you attending industry day (if there is one). Then it moves to you bringing on the right teaming partners or joining the right team.

It is a systematic process for making your company more and more competitive before or after the RFP is released.

To summarize, if you are a business developer that needs help doing this or you manage one or more business developers that need some help, there are two areas to focus on.

Do you have a list of metrics to evaluate whether you are doing the right activities and doing the right number of activities? And most important, how are you moving each opportunity through your pipeline, where every stage helps you become more and more competitive?

Take a step back. Think about how you are approaching business development and sales.

What are two or three things you can change, right now, to improve your win rate?

Something to think about.

Chapter 11.
Simplified Acquisitions

S implified Acquisition Procedures (SAP) is a subject often misunderstood by small businesses. Go to any conference or training session and everyone espouses how valuable they are for small business. Companies are running around looking for simplified acquisitions without understanding how they play into the larger scheme of acquisition strategy. To be clear, simplified acquisitions are awesome. If you are a small business, you need to understand them.

Simplified acquisition procedures fall under federal acquisition regulation 13, or FAR Part 13. The purpose of simplified acquisition is for the government to cultivate new contractors that may already be selling to the government or have not yet done so. They are specifically designed for small businesses.

The NDAA or National Defense Authorization Act has made some major changes to simplified acquisition. The micro-purchase threshold for the Department of Defense was increased in 2018 from $3,500 to $10,000 and federal agencies increased to $10,000.

But one of the most advantageous changes for small businesses is in the simplified acquisition threshold. It was increased from $150,000 to $250,000. This is a big deal for small companies.

I also want to point out that over the last ten years, federal appropriations and government spending has, for the most part, decreased. (Although the decrease in appropriations is like losing 100 mosquitoes in a yard with several million.) On the other hand, simplified acquisitions have increased every year in the last decade by close to a billion dollars a year.

One of the few consistent upwards trends, every year, has been simplified acquisitions and this is true even before the government increased the threshold from $150,000 to $250,000.

Simplified acquisition is not a contract vehicle like a firm fixed contract, a GSA Schedule, indefinite delivery indefinite quantity (IDIQ) contracts, or other multiple award contracts (MAC). Not to make a pun on words, but it is simply an acquisition *strategy*. It is not a contract vehicle.

To clarify, if it is full and open competition, it is competed under FAR Part 15. If it is released on GSA Schedule, it is competed under FAR Part 8.4. If you are a construction company, most architecture, engineering and construction contracts are competed under FAR Part 36. But if the agency or service wants to procure through simplified acquisition and give it to a small business, it is competed under FAR Part 13.

You can also use a GSA Schedule and other MACs as a contract vehicle for simplified acquisitions. There are many different combinations.

You want to understand that simplified acquisitions are steadily increasing as the government finds ways to simplify their buys.

So now that we have provided some background, let's talk about what you can do to take advantage of them. First, they are specifically for small business.

Have you ever noticed in SAM that there is what is called a "Combined Synopsis / Solicitation?" 60% to 80% of these are simplified acquisition. In other words, they are small business set-asides.

So, if you said, "Hey Josh, where do I find these?" One place is SAM.

Some of our clients and Federal Access members have said, "We don't want a $250,000 contract. We want to focus on $10 million contracts. I understand, but winning a simplified acquisition helps you build a relationship with the agency for larger contracts.

If you decide to go after simplified acquisitions (and the reality is many of you are probably bidding on them and not realizing it) you also want to attempt to position for a blanket purchase agreement (BPA).

You should absolutely ask contracting officers if they are willing to give you a BPA for simplified acquisitions. You also want to be aware that under a BPA, you can be awarded multiple contract actions… and *each action under simplified acquisition can be for $250,000*. If you get an agency or military command to award you a BPA and you get 8 or 10 orders, you could make over $2 million on that one BPA alone. Those small $250,000 contracts don't look so small now.

Last year, more than 70,000 small businesses had contract actions under simplified acquisition.

Talking to the agencies and asking questions about how and where they use simplified acquisitions is critical.

Let's provide some more clarity. Last year, over $20 billion was spent through simplified acquisition. So, even if only 50% of these are on SAM, that's still billions of dollars.

To successfully take advantage of simplified acquisitions, you need to think about how you are approaching government sales. Whether or not you create a plan to go after simplified acquisitions, at a minimum, you need to understand what they are, how and why the government uses them, and the opportunity for you to engage them.

Couple final points. Simplified acquisitions do not require a debrief. If you lose a simplified acquisition bid, the contracting officer is likely to say, "You lost. Someone else won. Thank you." Some contracting officers will simply ignore your emails and calls for a debrief. They are crazy busy and the federal acquisition regulation (FAR) *does not require that they debrief you.*

In my opinion, although you can find a percentage of simplified acquisitions on SAM, they are somewhat like the Small Business Administration's (SBA) All-Small Mentor-Protégé Program. You don't simply decide to do it and you are successful. Simplified acquisition requires that you have a strong business development strategy. It requires that you identify your annual core target agencies. You have to build relationships and focus 80% of your daily activities during pre-acquisition. By focusing on prospects before RFPs and RFQs are released, you are more likely to influence procurements.

As you build relationships, ask about their use of simplified acquisition, when they use them, and which contracting offices use them.

A strong business development strategy ensures that contracting officers know who you are. If they know who you are, you are more likely to learn of future simplified acquisitions as well as larger contract opportunities.

Build a strong metrics-based business development strategy. Identify your target agencies. Have conversations. Build relationships. Collect market intelligence. Simplified acquisition is nothing more than an acquisition strategy. You will gain more and more access to them as you strengthen your relationships and improve your market strategy.

Something to think about.

Chapter 12.
Finding Competitive Data on Existing Contracts

W hat do I do and where do I go to find intelligence on opportunities being recompeted? Where do I find information on existing contracts? Where do I find information and intelligence on agencies or military commands for new opportunities that are not recompetes? These are some of the most common questions that government contractors ask.

As I was updating this book for the second edition, I provided a training seminar at the SAME Small Business Conferences in Dallas, Texas. The highest attended session with more than three hundred small and large A/E/C companies, I gave a live demo of more than a dozen government websites and how to take data from one system and use it to find data in another system. NOTE [14]

Due to the amount of information, process, and Microsoft Excel pivot tables, my session was recorded for on-demand viewing post-event. It was an awesome session. I know several consultants that charge thousands for this capability and most of them won't teach you. They treat the process like the ingredients for Pepsi or Kentucky Fried Chicken and simply want to charge you for it... again and again. So in January 2020, we moved the on-

---

[14] Founded in 1920, the Society of American Military Engineers leads collaborative efforts to identify and resolve national security infrastructure-related challenges. With a National Office in Alexandria, Va., and more than 100 local Posts and Field Chapters around the world, the Society unites public and private sector individuals and organizations from across the architecture, engineering, construction, environmental and facility management, cyber security, and contracting and acquisition disciplines in support of America's national security. https://www.same.org/

demand video into the Federal Access Knowledge-Base. You can learn more about Federal Access at https://rsmfederal.com/FA.

Federal Access

Okay, let's take a quick time-out. I've already mentioned Federal Access several times in the book and it will be mentioned several more. I knew when I wrote this book that I wanted to provide more tactics and strategies on government sales than any book before it. For more than ten years I envisioned the value and power of giving these strategies to companies like yours.

In marketing parlance, business owners use CTAs or Calls to Action. There are several in this book. One of them is the Insider's Power Pack that I provide with free templates and strategies that you can download (only if you bought the book). Another CTA is the **Federal Access Knowledge-Base**. *It is NOT a bid-matching system*. It is hundreds of step-by-step strategies that cover all the chapters in this book; hundreds of professional graphics for your website and proposals; hundreds of training videos; and hundreds of templates for marketing, sales, teaming, proposals, and operations.

Yes, this book will help you accelerate your commercial and government sales! But it is just one resource. Remember what I said earlier about a job versus an occupation? An occupation is about life-long learning.

Federal Access is what gives you the tools to implement the strategies in this book. It is simply impossible to teach you these tactics and strategies and not tell you where these tools and templates can be found. Let me ask you a question. You find bid opportunities in SAM or your bid-matching system. Now what? How do you engage them? That's Federal Access. For $59 a month, you have access to every tool and resource you need to win government contracts. Oh, and it comes with a 100% money back guarantee.

Now you know why I refer to Federal Access.

* * *

Competitive intelligence. I'm often asked questions that involve:

- Who's the incumbent?

- Can I figure out who their team members are?

- What was the total value of the contract?

- Can I figure out the incumbent's labor rates?

- Can the incumbent go after the contract again?

- Is there any way I can figure out what the incumbent will use for pricing?

You may not be able to answer all these questions, but you should be able to answer many of them if you understand how to use the free and publicly available government data systems. Even more important, you need to understand *how to move back and forth between these systems*.

You will not be able to find contract data and information on every opportunity. It does not work that way. Government systems are 'garbage in - garbage out' (GIGO). Some contract data does not make it into the systems. Some contracting officers simply forget to enter the data. Some contracts, due to security, or from intelligence agencies, will not be available. It works between 60% and 70% of the time, which means you will not be able to find information on 3 or 4 out of every 10 opportunities you attempt to research. It is also possible (and often likely) that the data is there but you simply can't find it. This is normal, even for me.

This is why the most important thing you can do is identify the contract and solicitation numbers for the previous contract. Remember, the current solicitation number is almost always different from the one they used three, five, or ten years ago. So, you need the old solicitation and contract numbers.

First, I check FPDS / SAM because the advanced ad-hoc search functionality will give you the solicitation numbers!

If I can't find it in FPDS / SAM, I'll call the contracting officer and try to get the old numbers. As funny as it sounds, I often hear, "Sorry, I don't know the old number. I just took over and I have no idea where to find the old acquisition paperwork." Sometimes truth is stranger than fiction. This just proves that the government can be just as disorganized as the rest of us.

You can also ask the agency's small business office to research it for you. Every federal agency and every military service has a small business office. For the Department of Defense, they are called the Office of Small Business Programs (OSBP). For federal agencies, they are called the Office of Small

Disadvantaged Business Utilization (OSDBU). Some small business offices will find the contract and solicitation numbers, but most will not. But you should still pull-out all the stops and ask the question.

Now, assume you cannot get an answer. No one will tell you the old contract or solicitation number and they will not tell you who the incumbent is. Now what?

Now you go to the **Federal Procurement Data System** (FPDS) - https://www.fpds.gov. You know the agency. The RFP says it will be awarded in May. Well, think it through logically. This means the company that wins the contract will probably start in May, June, or July. Note [15]

Search FPDS / SAM by agency and filter by date going back five years, focusing on May, June, and July. We are going back five years as an example. If the opportunity you are researching is a three-year contract, then go back three years.

You are likely to find half-a-dozen to a dozen major contract actions for this specific agency, command, or contracting office. When you review these contract actions, you may very well find the one that matches the description of the current sources-sought, draft solicitation, or RFP.

Some are pretty clear cut. Others, you will still be in the dark without the answers you need.

Let's add another wrinkle to our research. Sometimes, one agency is responsible for managing the contract of another agency. But this is not the norm. Think large multiple award contracts that are issued by one agency and used by other agencies. Obtaining information on task orders is difficult. Just something to be aware of.

Now that you have found the contract in FPDS / SAM, *you have identified the incumbent.*

At this point, I change systems. I go to the **System for Award Management** (SAM) and I search for that company's "Entity Information." If the company name is not very unique, you may get twenty or thirty

---

[15] FPDS is migrating into the Integrated Award Environment (IAE) and will be part of System for Award Management (SAM) in 2020.

results. How do you know which one is correct? The contract action in FPDS / SAM will tell you the company's address.

Even easier, when you are in FPDS / SAM, write-down the incumbent's global DUNS / SAMMI number. Then simply search by the DUNS / SAMMI number in SAM. NOTE [16]

You now know if they are a large business, a small business, 8a, woman-owned, veteran, service-disabled, HUBZone, etc.

Let's take a short pause. Let's assume that the contract we are researching is from a sources-sought (pre-acquisition before an RFP is released). The contract record in FPDS / SAM confirms that the current contract was competed as an 8a set-aside. Now, look-up the incumbent in SAM. You might find that they will graduate the 8a program in two months.

Now assume you are SBA 8a certified. This opportunity just became more qualified! You know that the incumbent is likely unable to bid on the contract again if it is released as an 8a set-aside. It is very difficult for an agency to remove contracts from the 8a program once a contract has been awarded 8a.

So, we know that once a company graduates the 8a program they are no longer authorized to compete on 8a contracts. Or can they? There is one situation where graduated 8a's are still allowed to bid-on and win 8a contracts. It is the 8a STARS contract vehicle and it is for information technology companies. Several of our clients have now graduated the 8a

---

[16] Every company must obtain a DUNS number before they are able to register in the System for Award Management. In March 2019, the government awarded a new contract to Ernst & Young LLP for a five year contract to replace the DUNS number with what is called the SAM Managed Identifier (SAMMI). Expect the government to move from DUNS to SAMMI in 2020 or 2021. Since every contract action is uniquely identified by a contractor's DUNS number, DUNS numbers will remain for old contracts and be mapped to the new SAMMI numbers. Nothing you have to worry about. This will all be done automatically either when you register in the SAM for the first time or it'll be automatically mapped for companies that have been operating in the market for years.

program but still have two or three years remaining on their 8a STARS contract.

It can be a bit confusing but the more you learn about government acquisitions, the better you will be at positioning for these contracts.

After reviewing their profile in SAM, I go to **their website**. I want to know how much business they do with the government and how they position in the market.

- Do they have any contract vehicles?

- Are they on any multiple award contracts (MAC)?

- Do they have a GSA Schedule?

- Do they refer to their teaming partners? Who are they?

- Are they a potential teaming partner for your company?

If they have a GSA Schedule (or I'm not sure), my next step is to visit the **GSA eLibrary** - https://www.gsaelibrary.gsa.gov and see if they have a schedule.

If you do not have a GSA Schedule, you should still be using the GSA eLibrary for competitive intelligence! In this example, the incumbent has a schedule. Using the GSA eLibrary, I now have their labor categories, labor rates, and product pricing.

But we are not done yet! Then *you go back to* **FPDS / SAM** and search *solely by their Global DUNS* number. Now you have *all the contract actions they have been awarded*, as a prime, for the last decade.

Just at the Integrated Award Environment (IAE) is becoming the new aggregator for SAM, FPDS, PPIRS, FBO, and other sites, there is another long-standing aggregator site called USASpending.gov. Most companies that cringe at using FPDS use USASpending.gov. Unlike FPDS / SAM, USASpending.gov aggregates not only FPDS data but other data including subcontracting data. So if you search USASpending.gov by the global DUNS number, you may also find contracts where this company subcontracted on other contracts. May find.

So when you're researching contracts awarded and past performance for another contractor, use FPDS / SAM but also do a quick check on USASpending.gov for subcontracting work.

How awesome is this? You might already be using these systems. Most of our clients and FA already are. But you need to understand how to see the forest through the trees. You need to understand how to move between systems, using data from one to find data in another.

So now you know who the incumbent is. You know the total value of their contract. You have confirmed through the system for award management (SAM) that they do or do not still have the certification or status required for the recompete contract. You have confirmed if they have other contracts with that agency. You now have their labor categories, labor rates, and product pricing.

What if you want to find out who is on their team? Sometimes it is easy. Other times it's hard.

While the incumbent's website may not say who is on their team, I always check for a press release. Some primes will enter their teammates in the press release. Some teammates (the subcontractors) will put out their own press release. This happens quite often.

I also Google the contract name. Many subcontractors will list the contracts on their website and it is fairly standard and expected for subcontractors to put the prime's name in parentheses after the contract name.

Now, the million-dollar question. What were the incumbent's labor rates and pricing for this *specific* contract? Many companies think this is impossible to figure out. Yes, it can be tough but I can normally get pretty close if the information is in FPDS.

Here is a quick example. It is a contract for a call-center. The sources-sought or RFP makes it clear in the scope of work that there will be two primary shifts, each eight hours long. The government tells you how many calls come into the call center.

Sometimes, the government will even tell you how many full-time employees (FTE) are currently on the contract. That makes it easier. But let's assume they do not tell you the number of FTEs. Using your expertise and knowledge, you look at the number of calls. You look at the number of shifts. You figure it will take 18 FTEs to run the call center.

You also know from FPDS / SAM or USASpending.gov that the total contract value for the five-year contract was $7.5 million.

Using this information, I can do the math and say, it looks like the labor rate for most of these positions is somewhere around $35 to $45 an hour.

Now, what did I not take into account? I did not account for the standard 2% to 3% annual price increase for the option years (years two through five). I also did not take into account that each shift will have a supervisor that has a higher labor rate than the call center technicians.

So, what I will try to do is find the contract actions in FPDS / SAM *for just one year.* That will tell me how much was obligated in a 12 month period. Now I can come pretty close to figuring out their labor rates.

What if you cannot find any contract data but you know the name of the incumbent. If the incumbent has a GSA Schedule, then just go straight to the GSA eLibrary and get their labor rates. Go into SAM, find their profile and write down their DUNS number. Take their DUNS number and enter it into FPDS to find all their prime contracts. You cannot find this level of information and intelligence in the commercial market. The government market is different. You just have to understand which systems to use and how to use them.

You can do it. You just have to think it through. It takes experience. It takes practice. The tactics and strategies in this chapter will get you started. If you want to watch me go through these websites in real-time, you'll find the on-demand video in Federal Access.

The most important lesson is that it is not which systems you use to collect your intelligence. *It is learning how to move back and forth between systems, taking data from one and using that data in another to get the next piece of information.*

When it comes to pricing and labor rates, you will not always find the data you need. But when you can, you can back-into the incumbent's pricing. Now you know the pricing required on the new contract to be competitive.

Something to think about.

Chapter 13.
Identifying Competitor Pricing

O kay, we have two more chapters on pricing. So let's take this a step
further. Another common question I receive is, "How do I figure out
what my competition is charging?"

This chapter takes what we discussed in the last chapter and makes it a
bit more granular.

In this chapter, we are going to discuss where you find pricing
information on current contracts and the pricing that your competitors
charge. Even if you are familiar with these systems, actually having
someone walk through it can help show you how to take data from one
system and use it in another system.

Try as I can, I have not successfully found a way for you to watch a
video *inside this book*. So, if after you have read this chapter you still want to
watch a step-by-step video of this process, jump into Federal Access
https://rsmfederal.com/FA.

I am going to provide an overview of which websites I use. General FYI -
if I ran through every resource for researching pricing, this book would be
another thirty pages. I want to outline the ones I use the most often and
provide some pointers on how to use them.

Some of you may be using other tools to identify pricing or contract
values. If it is a really good site or tool and you feel I should have listed it,
let me know.

First, let's set expectations. Most companies look for three things:

1) Existing contracts. What is the contract value and is there a way
   to figure out how the incumbent priced the contract?

2) What are the labor rates for our competition?

3) For product sales, what are companies charging for twenty-five, a hundred, or a thousand units?

Most of the time, you can find ~ 70% of what you are looking for. Sometimes you will find everything you need. Other times, you will not find anything. As discussed in the previous chapter, it is hit or miss. But, if the information is out there, I am going to show you several ways of finding it.

If you are looking for contract information, specifically pricing and contract values, you are not likely to find it for the intelligence community. While not impossible, it is highly difficult. So, the CIA, DIA, NGA, NRO, etc. - you can try to find contract information, but you are more than likely going to have to focus on general labor categories and labor rates.

For federal agencies and military commands, when I am looking for contract values, product prices, or the labor rates being used by the competition, I quickly move between several different websites. They are all free. These sites include:

- Google

- DLA's Internet Bid Board System (DIBBS)

- Federal Procurement Data System (FPDS) Note [17]

- USASpending.gov

- GSA Advantage

- GSA eLibrary

- Cage Code Search Tool

- Department of Veterans Affairs National Acquisition Center; and

- Contract-Awarded Labor Category (CALC) tool.

---

[17] FPDS is migrating into the Integrated Award Environment (IAE) and will be part of System for Award Management (SAM) in 2020.

Let's jump in and walk through several examples. You know the name of your competitor. The name of their company is Enterprise Information Systems, Incorporated. What is their pricing? How competitive is your pricing? NOTE [18]

Step one is going to the **System for Award Management** (SAM). SAM provides much more value than you simply registering for government sales. It definitely has more value now that it is being integrated as part of the overall Integrated Award Environment (IAE). There is a lot of competitive intelligence you can obtain on other companies. When I look them up, I verify I have the right company by checking their address. Once I have verified that I have the right company, I write down their **DUNS / SAMMI number**. In this case, their number is 877501676.

Now I go to the **Federal Procurement Data System** (FPDS) / SAM. I search using their DUNS number. I find several contracts and I pick one at random. The contract value is $1,164,288.

Based on what I find in FPDS / SAM, they appear to have a GSA Schedule. So, I leave FPDS / SAM and go to the **GSA eLibrary**. The eLibrary is where all GSA Schedules are listed. Most schedules include labor categories and pricing. I head over to the GSA eLibrary.

I start searching by the company name. I find that they have a GSA Schedule. I download their "terms and conditions" and I immediately see their approved government pricing. Now, my objective is to identify what they charge for a junior system's analyst. I am fairly confident I will be competing against them on an opportunity with the Department of the Interior (DOI) which released a sources-sought last week.

When it comes to labor categories, there are normally a dozen different titles for any position. I am looking for 'systems analyst' or something similar. I find a 'Junior Program / Systems Analyst' with a government approved rate of $70.22 per hour.

But wait, is that really the pricing they use? Many companies do *not* use their approved GSA Schedule rates. They bid two to five points lower.

---

[18] An actual company in the System for Award Management. I have no relationship with them and I picked them at random for illustration purposes.

Why? Because the government has negotiated the rates for all similar companies. As a result, many companies drop their rates in order to be more competitive.

Furthermore, it is fairly common for the government to recommend in the RFP or RFQ that contractors provide pricing that is less than their approved rates. I could keep going down this rabbit hole but you get the picture.

Let's assume five points. That takes their pricing from $70.22 down to $66.71. Now you have a fairly decent 'guestimate' of what they are charging for this labor category. Now, for you to be competitive, I would drop the pricing by another two points. To be competitive, you need to charge $65.38 per hour for a junior systems analyst. This is not an iron-clad process. It is simply a strategy.

Published Labor Rates vs Acceptable Margins
Knowing that most companies bid 3 to 5 points below their government negotiated rates, not only must your pricing be in that lower range, it must be a point or two below the lowered range AND you must ensure that you have enough margin at that price!

You need to understand the risks and impacts of this strategy. Sometimes you will win. Other times you will lose. You may even win a contract and then find out that you gave away too much margin; that your guestimate of your competitors pricing was too low. *That is business*. If you won the contract but find out your pricing was too low, then bid a higher rate on the next proposal. Use the data at your disposal. Make decisions. Learn from your decisions and then adjust.

Now, let's say it is not a recompete. It is an entirely new requirement and contract. What if I am brand new to government sales and I want to identify average labor rates for various labor categories? The answer is the system for **Contract Awarded Labor Category** (CALC) managed by the General Services Administration (GSA).

Continuing with the example of a junior analyst, I go to CALC and search for junior analyst. The system will start auto-completing your search string. So as soon as I type 'junior' there will be several different labor categories to choose from. Once I select junior analyst, it gives me the average labor rate for all companies that have that labor category on their GSA Schedule. CALC is one of the best pricing research tools for general labor rate information and it searches all schedules for all industries.

So, that is a quick example of researching competitor pricing for service contracts. But what if you sell product? Let's run through an example.

Let's use power drills as an example. One of our clients sells power drills used for construction. The first website I go to is **GSA Advantage**. GSA Advantage only lists products for those companies that have a GSA Schedule. Even if you do not have a schedule, *you can still check the competitiveness of your pricing against your competition*. If you search for drills, you will get hundreds of results. Find the same drills you sell and you will know the competitive range. Easy.

Here is another great example. Let's say the manufacturer of your drill is the George Ficher Company. Every company has what is called a **CAGE Code**. It is assigned by the Department of Defense and you probably know your code. If you don't, go back through your emails. Remember when you registered in the System for Award Management (SAM)? Immediately following your registration, you were emailed a CAGE code.

But I digress. You do not need your code. *You need George Ficher's code.* There is a website for this! Just Google 'CAGE Code Search Tool." This is not a government website. It is privately operated but is free to use. Type in George Ficher and you will learn that their CAGE Code is 14889.

Now this is where understanding **DLA's Internet Bid Board System (DIBBS)** makes finding pricing data worthwhile. Now that you know the manufacturer's CAGE Code, you can search all active procurements that involve George Ficher products. Additionally, for every product you find, you will *also see the pricing that the government paid to other contractors* on the last several procurements.

Finally, if you see an RFP or RFQ that says pricing falls under the Service Contract Act (SCA), what does that mean? It means that your labor rate must, at a minimum, be no lower than the wage determination identified by the Department of Labor (DOL). NOTE [19]

To summarize, there is no right way to find competitive pricing information. Sometimes you will find what you need. Sometimes you will only find pieces. But you can always identify the competitive price points for your labor categories or the products you sell.

If you noticed, I often took information from one website and used it to find information in another. I went to SAM to identify the DUNS / SAMMI number and used the DUNS / SAMMI number to look in FPDS / SAM.

I used the Cage code lookup website to find the cage code for searching in DIBBS.

It will take a little time for you to figure out how to use each system and how to best utilize them. For what you sell, product or service, you will find that some sites are more useful than others.

Remember, sometimes you are not going to find what you are looking for. Many companies use bid-matching or contract management tools. Yes, they can help you with your capture or business development process. But even the most popular bid-matching tools obtain a majority of their data from the systems I just outlined. Yes, you can pay extra to access task order and advanced pricing information but you are still unlikely to get everything you want. If your company is on multiple indefinite delivery indefinite quantity (IDIQ) contracts and your primary focus is on task orders, then your company may want to consider paying extra for those add-ons. But make sure you ask the right questions, what you really want, before forking over the big bucks.

Finding intelligence on competitive single award contacts is not that difficult. Finding competitive intelligence on task orders or contracts with the intelligence community is like looking into a black hole.

The more you work with these systems, the more you understand how valuable they are.

---

[19] The Department of Labor's (DOL) rates under the Service Contract Act (SCA) are now fully integrated into the new Integrated Award Environment (IAE) or what most of us think of as the System for Award Management (SAM).

Do you use these systems? Do you want to be more competitive?

Something to think about.

Chapter 14.
Your Competitive Price Point (CPP)

C ontinuing our discussion from the last couple chapters, the lesson in
this chapter is the result of recent discussions with several of our
clients and their sales teams.

Do you have a process to validate if your pricing is competitive? There
are many terms for identifying your competitive pricing. I call it the
Competitive Price Point (CPP).

The competitive price point is often a frustrating exercise where many
companies either guess or ignore it. For example, combining the cost of
your employees, fringe benefits, overhead, corporate general and
administrative (G&A) costs, and profit is what is called your fully burdened
rate, or WRAP rate.

If your fully burdened rate is higher than the market average because
your overhead and G&A is too high; or you are dead-set on having 35%
margins even if other companies are going with 20%, then there is very little
you can do to be competitive. It doesn't matter how much margin you *want*.
It matters what the market is *willing to give* you.

If your fully burdened rates are higher than the competition, you only
have several choices. You have to minimize costs; you have to decrease your
overhead; decrease your margins; or you choose not to bid.

You have to accept the fact that other companies in your industry are
bidding with lower overhead. This allows them to bid lower and / or create
higher profit margins. If you have too many employees and it is increasing
your overhead, there is not much you can do. You can either reduce
overhead or lower your margins.

Your competitive price point is *not your standard pricing*.

A competitive price point is the pricing you have to submit to be competitive and to win a contract. Your competitive price point is different for *every opportunity*.

We all know that pricing is an exercise that you get better at the more often you do it. It is not as simple as saying, "this is what we charge" because your price points increase or decrease based on a wide range of criteria. These criteria may include the customer, how much competition you have, how much the customer has paid in the past for similar products or services, and what your competition charges.

Your competitive price point may also be influenced by the time of year. Is it the first quarter or last quarter of the fiscal year when some companies are dropping their rates in a fire sale to make up for lost sales?

Most companies have a formal process for identifying what they will charge for their products and services. But many companies use an informal process for how they bid on proposals. Both of these should be formal processes.

It is also important to note that very few companies actually use their government approved rates. I'm talking about GSA Schedules, multiple award task order contracts, and almost all other contracting vehicles. I discussed the reasons why companies drop their government approved pricing by two to five points in the previous chapter.

You need a formal process for identifying what pricing you will use on every proposal or bid. You cannot simply say, "This is our approved pricing and this is what we are going to use." *That is a recipe for disaster.*

Calculating your competitive price point for a bid is done at the same time that the proposal is being developed.

Someone, normally the business developer, the individual that has the lead on winning the opportunity, is responsible for identifying the competitive price point. But for many companies, the business developer is not the person who puts the pricing together. There is often a handoff. The business developer or proposal writer drafts the response and sends it to someone else who cleans it up and adds the pricing.

This individual could be a sales manager, the CFO, or the CEO.

It might be you.

And this is where I want to focus the rest of this chapter. Every time you forward a draft proposal to someone in the company for review, you also need to *forward your best-guess on the competitive price point.*

Here is an example. You are the business developer or proposal writer and you draft a proposal. You forward the draft to management who says, "we need 35% margin so I'm going to charge $100,000 for this work."

In most companies, no one bats an eye. Everyone is thinking "Yep, pricing looks good. Let's hope we win," and then they lose the bid because they were much higher.

This is often when you hear a company say, "Oh B.S.! That's impossible! No one can do the work for that little. We need to protest."

If it's a procurement for product, you will hear companies say, "Absolutely impossible. What they charged is 6% less than the pricing we get from the manufacturer."

If you do not have a formal process for identifying the competitive price point, you are probably responding like this just before you ask for a debrief.

So, what are some of the ways to identify competitive price points? First, use USASpending.gov and the Federal Procurement Data System (FPDS) / SAM. Look up companies that have won contracts with that specific customer or agency in the last 12 months, that sell what you sell.

If it is a recompete for an existing contract, get the contract number and use USASpending.gov or FPDS / SAM to look up the base year value or last option year value.

Google the company and the customer and see if the incumbent put out a press release with a dollar value. There are many ways to find contract values for your competition or pricing for existing contracts. For more detail and a step-by-step process, refer to the previous chapter on Identifying Competitor Pricing.

Every opportunity that you attempt to win has a unique competitive price point. It is just as important as the technical portion of your proposal. If you have lost many of your recent bids because of pricing, then you need a stronger process for pricing that includes identifying the competitive price point.

For many small companies, the CEO or President does the pricing. That is normal. But it is not okay if the fully burdened rates they use do not take the competitive price point into account! So, if you are not the one that does the pricing, you want to make sure that you do this research and *give it to the person that is responsible for pricing*.

If you are the one responsible for pricing, do not let anyone forward you a draft of the proposal or bid without them first researching the competitive price point.

Never accept a draft proposal without the recommended competitive price point. This will make you more competitive!

Close is good enough. You need a best guestimate. Do not worry about being too high or too low. Some you will win and others you will lose. The more pricing, cost data, and labor rates you can find, the more accurate you will be.

If you don't do this, you will bid a million dollars on a contract and find out the winning bid was $800,000. Every proposal or bid requires some level of research to guestimate the competitive price point for that specific opportunity.

For products and commodities, make sure you create an account with the Defense Logistics Agency's (DLA) Internet Bid Board System (DIBBS). Billions of dollars in procurements go through DIBBS every year. For DIBBS RFQs, the government tells you the last several times they bought that product, how many they bought, and the total price for the procurement. It is one of the few government systems that provides this level of granular pricing detail. If you sell product, check it out!

The competitive price point is a formal process you must build into every proposal / bid cycle. Sometimes, you will find the data and intelligence you need. Other times you won't find anything. But you are not going to win many contracts if you don't do it.

Something to think about.

Chapter 15.
Low Price Technically Acceptable (LPTA)

T *he bane of your existence*. Nothing is more frustrating than bidding on an opportunity to then realize the competitive price is with a 0.5% margin. To be clear, that's less than 1% margin! Over the years, I have had this discussion with hundreds of companies.

Let's talk about Low Price Technically Acceptable (LPTA) contracts.

We recently had Bill Thoet with GovBizConnect as a guest speaker on our Podcast *Game Changers For Government Contractors*. If you are interested in better understanding LPTA, you can listen to Bill's and other Game Changers podcasts. They are free on Soundcloud and iTunes. https://federal-access.com/game-changers/

I am going to cover three areas of interest.

- why the government uses LPTA

- how the government evaluates LPTA bids; and

- how you should position, influence, and compete

First, there is no magic to LPTA procurements. For LPTA bids, how you *run your business* directly impacts how competitive you are going to be.

You know your company's financial challenges and limitations. Companies that win LPTA contracts can afford to have slim margins.

Let's start with why the Government uses LPTA. Over the last 12 years, LPTA contracts have become fairly popular. Let's take the Department of Defense (DoD) as an example. 20 years ago, DoD had $250 billion in appropriations (budget) and the overall federal market had more than 100,000 contracting officers and contracting specialists.

Today, DoD has more than tripled appropriations to more than $700 Billion and the overall federal market has dropped from 100,000 contracting officers and contracting professionals to somewhere between 30,000 and 40,000 contracting professionals.

Appropriations have more than doubled or tripled and the acquisition community has decreased by more than half. Is it any surprise that the government is trying to simplify procurements?

On top of this, Sequestration, which is supposed to decrease spending by more than a $1 trillion, although not implemented, remains on the books.

Now some good news before I dive into strategies and recommendations.

Because ~70% of contractors surveyed by *Washington Technology*[20] stated that LPTA bids have negatively impacted their businesses, the 2019 National Defense Authorization Act (NDAA) directs a more limited use of LPTA procurements by the government. The authorization act requires a supplement to the Federal Acquisition Regulation (FAR) to limit the use of LPTA to only the most straight forward product procurements. The NDAA also recommended that technology and other professional services *avoid* using LPTA procurements.

But these recommendations are analogous to the Government Accountability Office (GAO) recommending an agency cancel an acquisition due to a protest. Federal agencies and military commands do not have to follow GAO recommendations. So, for the NDAA, these are recommended changes until formally implemented. You could argue that the NDAA's guidance is in fact a mandate, *but who decides* whether any given procurement actually includes 'professional services?' What is the definition of professional services? Hmmm.

That's right - the contracting officer still gets to make the final decision. This is an excellent example where implementation of a government law or act is at the discretion of a decision maker.

LPTA contracts are not going anywhere.

_____

[20] https://washingtontechnology.com

Now, let's talk about what LPTA really means.

First, there is no incentive to exceed requirements. Whether or not your proposal is stronger than the competition is *not* an evaluation factor. You are either technically 'responsive' or you are not.

When it comes to an LPTA bid, the evaluation criteria are very straight forward. Everything other than price is evaluated on a pass or fail basis. It is not about exceeding the requirements or showing 'what you can do.' It is not about how well you can differentiate. It is not whether your past performance is stronger than the competition. It is simply pass or fail.

Once the agency has a stack of proposals that pass the technical evaluation, the one with the lowest price wins. Everyone is low-balling on price.

Your past performance could be one-hundred times stronger than everyone else but if your labor rate is $100 and the competition bids $99, you lose. This is the problem with LPTA contracts. This is also why industry screamed bloody-murder about using LPTA on technology and professional service contracts. Another reason why the NDAA is now mandating (recommending) that professional service contracts not use LPTA.

When you first submit your proposal, source selection will review your technical response. Yes, it is low price, but if you do not successfully meet the requirements and you fail the technical evaluation, price no longer matters. Yes, price is still going to make or break your success, but you will never get to the price evaluation if your bid does not pass the technical review. This assumes that the bid requires more than just pricing.

If you do not have a strong requirements traceability matrix (RTM), how do you know if you are being responsive to every requirement? Using an RTM is not just for LPTA bids. You want to use an RTM for every opportunity you engage. After you have completed pre-qualification of the opportunity and you know that you are going to bid on it, you need to create an RTM to ensure you understand every direct and implied requirement in the solicitation. How else will you know if your bid or proposal is fully responsive and answers every question and requirement?

Have you ever responded to a solicitation and received an email that said, "You have been removed from competition due to being non-responsive"? This means you failed to respond to requirements in the solicitation. It could be that your font size was too small, that you exceeded the page count, or that you forgot to respond to a requirement in the statement of work (SOW) or performance work statement (PWS). An RTM ensures that you are *responsive*.

Many companies minimize and streamline their RTM and then submit it with their proposal to prove to source-selection that they have responded to every requirement. An RTM is simply a list of all the requirements in the RFP or RFQ. When you write your proposal, you are checking-off each requirement against what you have written in your response. If you are looking for an RTM template, you can find a template in the Federal Access Knowledge-Base.

Allow me to go off on another tangent. Yes, there are software tools you can buy that will automatically read an RFP and spit-out out the requirements for you in an automated spreadsheet or report. Some of these are decent tools.

In my opinion, if I am going to respond to an RFP, I want to personally review every paragraph, every sentence, every word, to make sure I understand the requirements. I want to fully understand any 'implied' or 'perceived' requirements that may get missed and not identified by a software tool.

These tools are a great double-check. I am not old-fashioned. My company runs the Federal Access Knowledge-Base and Training Platform supporting more than 1,000 companies. We run some serious technology. But technology will never replace your brain (at least not in our lifetime). If you are going to use an online RTM software tool, **make sure that you can first do it without the tool**. Otherwise it is just a bad crutch to a misunderstood or missing process.

Now, let's talk LPTA strategy.

Your proposals need to focus on responding to requirements *with the value you provide*. Since the technical volume will simply be pass or fail, this has caused some contractors to focus on offering additional value and communicating innovation at lower price points.

Now, while you could communicate innovative approaches as a means of differentiating your response, *I recommend against it* unless you have spoken to the government prospect and you know they are open to it.

Focus on the value you provide. When it comes to innovation, in general, the government is fairly risk-adverse. Do not forget that most of the time an RFP or RFQ that is LPTA outlines exactly what they want. I know you want to show them how your services provide more value, but if you recommend services that will make your pricing even a little more expensive, you are going to lose. Give them what they want and do it in a way where your response meets the requirements *but is more credible*.

Here is a good example. A Department of Veterans Affairs (VA) hospital in Ohio released an RFP for a Wi-Fi upgrade to support the patient rooms and family waiting areas. Their current Wi-Fi system is an old system. They wanted bids on updating the current system. The RFP discussed three of the pieces of hardware that were not providing the level of capability they should. They asked industry to fix their system. If the VA really wanted to properly update their system, they would need to replace all the hardware, not just the three pieces they asked for. By replacing all the hardware, the VA's Wi-Fi system would be ten-times faster, last five years longer, and would save the VA thousands of dollars in future repair and upgrade costs.

One company bid to replace the three pieces of hardware for $6,000. The other company made an outstanding business-case for how a full revamp of the system would improve their system and save them money in the long run. They bid $65,000.

The solicitation was clearly identified as LPTA. Guess who won? The moral of this story is to give the government what they want. The time to *influence the acquisition* is not after the RFP or RFQ has been released. Sometimes, we get so excited about how good we are at what we do and knowing what the client really needs, that we allow our expertise to cloud our judgement. How about that? You being an expert at what you do may not be what the government wants!

At this point, you are thinking, "Well okay! I am not giving them anything they did not ask for!"

But there is at least one exception to this rule.

If you have a process, product, or solution that provides a game-changing value, then the trick is to *offer that value where it costs you little to nothing*!

What is an example of this? Whether you are a technology company, a construction company, a security company, or an environmental remediation company, you are going to quote a number of full-time employees (FTE) to perform the work.

You will likely have a project manager. You will have one or more technical or team leads. Using the solicitation, you are going to break down the services and value that each FTE will provide on the contract.

Now, your company has a back-office, right? There is an owner, a vice president, perhaps a manager or two? Have you ever considered telling the government (or commercial prospects for that matter) that:

"We have specifically designed a "reach-back capability" for emergencies, project challenges, and future innovative approaches?"

For example, your onsite team or even the government may require assistance on strategy, daily activities, recommendations, or project requirements? I am talking about the ability for your onsite team and the government to escalate challenges or issues to the senior management of your company.

In this example, when you submit your proposal with a line and block diagram for your team, you can put a dotted line between your project manager and your corporate headquarters. Then you show a 'cell' of individuals at your headquarters that are 'on call 24/7' to support your team. This is what the military calls reach-back capability. Examples of this template and graphic are in Federal Access.

Not only are you using government terminology, but you are providing additional value at little or no cost to you and *no additional cost* to the government. You might get one or two calls during a year-long project. If you are worried about getting flooded with issues by your onsite team, just make sure you have wisely selected your project manager or team lead.

You already have these people in your company. You are already paying their salaries. This is not smoke and mirrors. The reality is, ***you already have this built into how you operate today***! As an owner or senior manager, you already keep tabs on your people, right? Do you not keep in contact with your employees that are on various contracts? Do you not ask them for updates, ask if everything is okay, or help them and redirect resources when they need help?

So, here is the question. Are you communicating this value, one you provide anyway on every contract, and are you communicating it in your proposal? Reach-back is *just one example.* It may take some time to wrap your arms around this concept. But it is an outstanding concept to understand and employ.

Another common strategy on LPTA bids is to ghost what accurate pricing should be. Often times, when you lose an LPTA bid, your response may be:

"There is no human way they can successfully provide these products (with these specifications) or services at those price points. This is total B.S."

So, you need to show the government what it really takes to successfully accomplish the contract. Just as we discussed in Chapter 4, you need to 'ghost' their expectations.

You are ghosting and explaining requirements that may not have been directly outlined in the RFP or RFQ. You want to make sure that you identify products or services required to execute the contract that the government may not have thought of. Do not assume that the government knows what they really need. Set expectations with source selection that in the event you are a bit higher in cost than other companies, it is likely the other companies failed to account for a required piece of hardware or service. You are ghosting an expectation that there is no way the other bidders should be able to realistically or successfully execute the contract without that product or service.

So, if you believe your pricing is going to be slightly higher than the competition, consider ghosting an explanation in your technical response for why other companies may not have properly priced their bids. You want to do this 'softly.'

Due to these challenges, as part of your bid - no bid process, you want to consider whether or not the scope in the RFP or RFQ is highly defined. The more defined the requirements, the less likely another company will influence the acquisition. But this cuts both ways!

This goes against conventional wisdom, but I like LPTA opportunities where the scope is well defined *but not fully defined.* And guess what? A large number of LPTA bids fall into this category. A strong proposal can remind source selection of what should be a part of the pricing, even if the government did not ask for it. This allows me to bid a slightly higher price and win (maybe).

Don't make a practice of this. More times than not, you will lose the bid. This strategy should be used sparingly. I do not win because I have a higher price. Well, I do, but I win because the other contractor's bid, with the slightly lower price, *is no longer credible*!

When it comes to LPTA pricing, yes, your margins are going to be low. If you feel your bid is going to be average or slightly over in price, make sure the government knows why. Make it look like your competition did not take something into account. Successfully do this and your competition is no longer credible. I know, I'm beating a dead horse. But this is important, especially for companies that may have higher fully-burdened rates or manufacturer pricing.

Your first priority is to show the government you will do exactly what they want. Providing additional value, at no additional cost, could be a valid strategy to facilitate a perception of increased value or maturity. Do not go crazy where additional value takes center-stage in your response.

Couple final points.

For product companies, if you cannot get preferred pricing from the manufacturer, there is little you can do. This is very common. I'll say it again... this is very common. A couple years ago, I spoke at the Department of Veterans Affairs National Veterans Conference. I also attended a VA panel and companies were screaming bloody-murder about LPTA. I heard several companies stand-up and say:

"Hey VA, it's not fair. We cannot get decent pricing from manufacturers because we are either too small or don't do enough business with these manufacturers."

That is not the VA's fault. That is simply business. As much as you want to bid and win contracts, you either have a relationship with a manufacturer or you don't. If you cannot be competitive on price, move on. Stay away from LPTA procurements.

Also, LPTA contracts are no different than best value contracts when it comes to business intelligence. If the first time you see the opportunity is when it is released on SAM and you have no prior information or intelligence, your level of competitiveness is pretty much the same for LPTA as it would be for best value opportunities. Some other company will have intelligence that will influence the acquisition.

In other words, "did you influence the acquisition before the RFP was released? If there was a sources-sought, did you respond to it? Did you call the government to ask questions before the RFP was released?

Even if you influence the acquisition before the RFP is released; even if you ghost pricing factors into your proposal to minimize the credibility of your competition; and even if you slash your margins, you are still competing against the fully burdened rates of your competition.

If your overhead, G&A, and overall operating costs are higher than industry average, then it may not matter how low your margin is.

If you are interested in identifying the average fully burdened rates for your industry, just visit the GSA eLibrary and CALC. Find your competition and look at their labor categories and labor rates. You sell products? Go look on GSA Advantage.

If you are the incumbent contractor and your original contract was competed best-value and then the recompete is LPTA, you are in serious trouble. There is no sugar-coating this and there is little you can do to fight it. You are in trouble because your pricing will force you to create a level of flexibility you do not have. Your labor rates will likely require major cuts to salaries, benefits, and other promises you have made to your employees. The exception is if you have large margins on another contract that allows you to bid at lower rates than what you bid the first time around.

Bidding an LPTA contract requires that you carefully focus on your business, making sure your overhead and costs are as low as possible. It requires that you understand your competition and what their price points are likely to be. You can check GSA eLibrary for your competition's rates and use FPDS / SAM or USASpending.gov for previous contract award values.

To summarize, there are a minimum of three strategies you should consider.

One, **manage and control business expenses**. Do not let your fully burdened rates automatically take you out of competition. This is the most important! If your rates are higher than the competition because of the direct, indirect, fixed, and variable costs of running your business, there may be little you can do to be competitive.

Two, focus on **communicating additional value**. Use resources and value you provide anyway and convince the government your solution is stronger.

And last, **make sure every price point is explained** so that companies that bid unrealistically low prices are viewed as not being credible.

So, what are you going to change about how you approach LPTA opportunities?

It starts with your expenses and how you run your company!

LPTA bids may not be for you.

Something to think about.

Chapter 16.
Preparing for Government Q4

Y ou have heard it before. To be successful in Q4, you must do "these" three or four things. If you are a member of RSM Federal's Federal Access Knowledge-Base and Training Platform, you know that you need to lay a foundation in Q1, Q2, and Q3.

Why does everyone focus on Q4? Because billions of dollars are obligated in the final two months of the government fiscal year. These are the months of August and September.

There's no magic to winning contracts in Q4.

You need to build a strong pipeline of opportunities that are a mix of you both priming and subcontracting. You want the opportunities in your pipeline to be worth 4 to 5 times your annual sales target. If your company's sales goal is $5 million, then you need $20 to $25 million in *qualified* pipeline opportunities. If you need help on this, go back to the Chapter 9 on *Do You Have Enough Opportunities in Your Pipeline*?

Now here is the question: Where should you be spending 80% of your time during the year? The answer is pre-acquisition. Pre-acquisition is engaging government buyers before an RFP is released without necessarily focusing on specific opportunities.

To best prepare for Q4, you have to do the right activities at the right times throughout the rest of the year.

You know deep down that to take advantage of Q4 you have to position in Q1, Q2, and Q3.

But let's say you are 120 days, four months from the end of the fiscal year. What should you be doing? I am going to provide several recommendations. There are two core activities you should be doing right now and they are no different than what you should be doing the rest of the year.

Your Acquisition Options

First, make a list of your acquisition options. Make sure that government buyers know *how to buy from you*. Do you have a GSA Schedule? Are you a small business? Are you certified 8a? Woman owned? Veteran owned? Are you the prime or a subcontractor on a multiple award task order contract (MATOC) or an indefinite delivery indefinite quantity (IDIQ) that one or more agencies use?

Do you have any blanket purchase agreements (BPA) with a targeted agency that can use that BPA? Make sure they know you accept credit cards. Double-check your profile in the System for Award Management (SAM) to ensure you did not pass over this, that it confirms you accept credit cards.

Even though the micro-purchase threshold is currently $10,000 for federal agencies and the Department of Defense, *I have seen government buyers drop $40,000 on a credit card two hours before the end of the fiscal year*. In Q4, some government buyers will create the justification to put larger contracts on a credit card.

Now, if you are a small business and you have no other small business status or GSA Schedule, then your focus is making sure that government buyers know who you are and that you have quality products and services with strong past performance. Your past performance may all be commercial. That's okay.

Let's say your company provides change management consulting services and you are woman-owned and SBA 8a (minority / socially disadvantaged) certified. You have a GSA Schedule and you accept credit cards. Update your capability statement with a section titled *Acquisition Options* and how they can buy from you.

You might say,

"We understand federal acquisition and recognize the government's role in validating acquisition strategy. At times, the government is pressed to accelerate procurements to meet internal agency requirements. In these situations, our company is positioned to support these requirements. When working with federal

agencies, the government has leveraged the following procurement strategies for our products and services:

- *Purchase Card (Micro-purchases)*

- *8a Sole Source*

- *WOSB Sole Source*

- *GSA Schedule with 8a Sole Source*

- *GSA Schedule with WOSB Sole Source*

- *Blanket Purchase Agreements via 8a and WOSB*

- *Blanket Purchase Agreements with our GSA Schedule.*

That's more than half-a-dozen ways for the government to buy from you! Notice that I did not list 8a set-aside or WOSB set-aside. Why? Because if they decide not to sole-source, they will probably set-aside anyway. Seems trivial, but do not float the option unless you have to.

Never assume that they know your acquisition options. They are too busy and when they need to make a decision, they are not going to remember options for your company unless you have spelled them out.

I often hear, "But Josh, my website and capability statement already have this information." That is true but many companies *do not list their acquisition options*. What you have on your capability statement and website are your certifications, not the acquisition options that can be used to buy from you.

This is not semantics. This is very important. Educating your buyers on the multiple and combined options they have for your products and services is smart strategy.

So, the first core activity in preparing for Q4 is to *help the government buy from you*. Not only should you list acquisition options on your capability statement, you should also include an "acquisition support section" in *every* sources-sought that you respond to. This is not just for Q4! **You should be doing this in every sources-sought response throughout the year.** I hope you highlighted this.

I can imagine some lightbulbs going off as you consider this strategy. Many small companies have a status. Some have a GSA Schedule. Most accept credit cards. Make it easy for the government to see how easy it might be to buy from you when it is September 29th and there are only 24 hours left in the fiscal year.

If you think the idea of winning a government contract on the last day of the fiscal year is far-fetched, consider these numbers. In the final week of a recent fiscal year, there were 155,000 contract actions. Wow! That is just in the final week! On September 29th, forty-eight hours from end of fiscal year, there were 29,000 contract actions. And on September 30th, the final day of the fiscal year when the government must allocate all remaining dollars, there were 10,000 contract actions!

Here is another fascinating point. The 30th was a Saturday. That is *10,000 contract actions on a Saturday*. It is the one day of the year when the government will be working on the weekend in full-force.

Most of these transactions were purchase orders and contracts awarded to companies that educated government buyers and built relationships with them. *The government knew who they were* and understood *how to quickly and easily procure their products and services*. Being listed in the System for Award Management (SAM) is not enough. Having visited a prospect six months ago is not enough. Having a GSA Schedule is not enough. You have to build and cultivate relationships. They have to know who you are. They have to remember you. Relationships are so critical that as I write this, I can't help but not think of Mark Amtower. Mark, known as the "Godfather of Government Marketing," is one of the strongest proponents of relationship marketing in the government space. If you are not connected with him on LinkedIn, you should be. He's one of the market's pioneers. Your highlighter should be out again. Connect with both of us on LinkedIn. In your connection invite, tell Mark I said to connect with him.

Quick side note. When I released the first edition of this book, I didn't tell Mark that I included him in the book or that I had recommended folks connect with him. Mark didn't learn about it until after several folks connected and said, "Josh's book said to connect with you." Guess what? Mark and I are now collaborating on projects for the upcoming year. Small world. Relationships are kind of important.

Focus on Pre-Acquisition

The second core activity for taking advantage of Q4 is *focusing on pre-acquisition*.

Let's define pre-acquisition again. Pre-acquisition are those activities that you take before the government has notified industry that an acquisition is going to take place or it is a sources-sought or draft solicitation on SAM. Whether you are reading these chapters in order or you are jumping around, you will notice that I keep coming back to pre-acquisition.

Focusing on pre-acquisition means you are focused on the relationships you build with government buyers and *not* simply looking for and bidding on SAM or other bid-matching opportunities.

However, if you are a small business, you absolutely want to continue looking for small business set-asides and sole-source opportunities. Why? Because focusing on pre-acquisition also means you are focusing on *"influencing the acquisition"* … not simply reacting to procurements you find on SAM. But until you build the necessary relationships, you need to continue your tactical approach on engaging SAM opportunities.

No matter how strong your strategy may be, if you don't bid, you don't win.

You need to build and strengthen your relationships with government buyers. Using the same hypothetical timeline as we discussed earlier, let's assume we are 120 days, four months, from end of fiscal year. You are going to have relationships but probably not as many as you would like. So, first things first. Consistently and aggressively engage the government buyers you know.

From a business perspective, the average company increases their revenue by 50% with new contracts *from past and current clients*. If you have some, give extensive focus to your current government customers.

If your company is like many small businesses, you may not have enough relationships and regardless of Q4, *you cannot rectify that overnight*. Selling to the government also requires that you set realistic expectations for you and your company.

Pick up the phone and start making calls. It does not have to be hard and you do not have to make it complicated. Using the Federal Procurement

Data System (FPDS) / SAM or USASpending.gov, identify who buys what you sell, how much they buy, and how often they buy it (Propensity). Call the top 50 government buyers of your products and services. Introduce yourself and start collecting market intelligence. Just start asking questions.

When you are done with the initial call, send a tailored capability statement based on your conversation. List your acquisition options that the government can use to quickly and easily buy from you. Put these in the body of your email as well.

Then when it is July, contact them twice. Once by email and once by phone.

In August, call them twice. Stay in front of them. Make them remember you. If you cannot get them on the phone, then send emails. Do it softly and somewhat informally. Do not stalk them. Use a soft approach without being pushy. You are just ensuring they know who you are, *the value you provide*, and the options they have for buying from you.

Stay in front of them.

Then in September, call or email them every week.

Stay in front of them.

If you are worried about being perceived as a stalker – don't. This is part of positioning in Q4. It is business.

It can be as simple as saying, "Hi Mary, it's Janet Williams with ABC Incorporated. Just making sure I didn't miss something on SAM. Wanted to make sure I don't miss any requirements."

That's it. You have already had the initial marketing push. You have already told them how you can support their requirements. They know your acquisition options.

Stay in front of them.

Now, if you are a product company, you are always having sales throughout the year. Don't use the same promotion you just used for your commercial clients. You can, but you need to tailor it specifically for the government. Instead of only emailing and calling in August and September, create a promotion and put it on a one-page marketing slick.

Between July and September, you may be giving government customers a three-point discount on all procurements over $5,000 and a five-point discount on all procurements over $15,000.

Yes, you will take a hit to your margin, which you need to ensure you can accept, but you may get several orders because your pricing is now stronger than the competition. The competitiveness of your pricing may have nothing to do with it. It may simply be that you stayed in front of them!

And last, pay attention to your teaming strategy. Just like you are creating a plan to engage the government, you need a plan for engaging your partners and prospective partners. Not some, "Oh, I have an opportunity. I need a teaming partner. Hmmm. Who should I call this time?" You need a formal and well thought-out teaming strategy.

Stop. Read that last paragraph again. No, seriously. Highlight it. If you bring this book to an event and ask me to sign it, I swear I'm going to jump straight to this page and see if there are stars, smiley faces, and highlighter marks.

Engage all the companies you have spoken with in Q1, Q2, and Q3. In July, touch each of these companies at least once or twice. In August, touch them every two weeks. In September, reach out and contact them every single week.

Now you have the two core strategies for positioning for Q4 contracts. Educate government buyers with a list of acquisition options for your company and continue to focus on pre-acquisition activities with the recommendations and strategies listed above.

There are thousands of coaches, consultants, counselors, and small business specialists. Every single one has an opinion on what it takes to "win in Q4." Most of their guidance is solid. But most of their guidance flows into one single truth -

A successful Q4 is dependent on how you position during the rest of the year!

Something to think about.

Chapter 17.
Marketing a Capability You Don't Have

L et's start with a couple of my favorite quotes from other business professionals. "Luck is what happens when preparation meets opportunity [21]," and *"You are an expert at whatever you decide to be an expert at."*

Many small business owners, and their employees, have an ethical tug-of-war when it comes to saying what their company can or cannot sell or the services they *can* perform.

Here is an example: You are a staffing company, a technology company, or any other service company that has never won a prime government contract. However, your company subcontracts on two government contracts.

You have 10 full time employees (FTE) supporting a helpdesk / call center for the Department of the Interior (DOI) and another 20 FTEs supporting a contract with Health and Human Services (HHS). For the last three years, you have had 30 employees subcontracting on two different contracts.

But now you want to prime.

You have the office space. Your company has two floors in your building. Right now, everyone works on the first floor. The second floor is storage and a couple of conference rooms. You have enough extra desks (or tables) and chairs to support a 25-person call center.

---

[21] Quote by Elmer Letterman

You have the past performance. Even though you are a subcontractor on your current contracts, your employees on these contracts absolutely count as past performance.

But here is the challenge. You have never primed a call center contract. You do not have a call center phone system and you do not have the software to run a call center operation. On top of this, you do not have any in-house recruiters to find the people to fill these positions.

In this example, the business owner wants to bid on a call center opportunity as the prime. The owner tells their business developer and / or proposal manager to "make it happen." On too many occasions to count, I have heard employees say:

"Josh, I know what the president wants, but we really can't do this. We have never done this before! We do not have the phone system or software! How can we tell the government that we are fully capable of performing this contract? We are not prepared to run a call center. We do not have a call center!"

While all of this may be true, there is a reason that this employee is an employee and not the owner of the company. He needs to understand how businesses grow. Business owners will stop at nothing to grow their companies.

Smart business professionals understand *how to market future capability*.

I had a lengthy discussion with the business manager for one of our clients. He was adamant that the owner was stretching the company too far. He felt uncomfortable telling the government that they were qualified and ready to execute a call center contract. He was concerned that the company could not execute the contract.

He agreed that the company had strong past performance. But they did not have an in-house call center; did not have the technology required; and did not have a strong enough staff of recruiters to fill the positions if they won the contract.

I call this the 'small business mindset.' If you do not think strategically; if you do not think you can win; if you do not think you are fully capable, then *there is no way you are going to win the contract.* Having a small business mindset is like a red-neon sign in your proposal. It screams "we're not ready!"

How do you think companies with in-house call centers won their first contract? Did they have the software, staffing, or telecommunications before they won their first contract? Most did not!

In this example, you have outstanding past performance. Okay, so you need to build-out your center. From a planning perspective, a strategic perspective, what will it take?

Part of your thought process is identifying the cost. You make several calls. You learn that it is $1,300 a month for the phone lines. It is another $1,200 a month for the call center software. It is $500 for each laptop.

The cost of building-out a call center in your existing office space has a fixed cost for the laptops of $12,500. Your costs for phone lines and software is another $30,000. Total cost to have a fully operational call center is around $43,000 for year one.

That is a lot of money! For many small businesses, you are never going to tie up your cash without having a contract. And that is the catch-22 that many companies do not understand.

Is it a catch-22?

No.

Think in business terms.

Here are some example numbers. 25 Call center employees at $50 an hour. That is a $2.5 million revenue stream for year one.

Assume you have $5 margin on each FTE. At 1920 hours, that's $9,600 a year profit *per FTE*.

Your total profit *each year* is $240,000. It is a three-year contract so your profit is $720,000 over the life of the contract.

It will cost $43,000 to stand-up the call center. Another $30,000 per year in year's two and three for phone and software. Total cost for all three years is around $103,000. That is 14.3% of your total three-year profit. Instead of making $720,000 over three years, you are making $617,000. You are still making more than half-a-million dollars!

This is simply the price of doing business.

When I walk through this with clients, a light-bulb goes off. No matter their industry, they realize that they absolutely can quote a capability they do not currently have.

Even if you do not have extensive past performance, like in this example, you can still position your company to win a contract that you have never won before.

It can be a call center, a vertical construction project, or anything that you sell or *want to sell*.

Remember the earlier quote? "You are an expert at whatever you decide to be an expert at."

This is how small companies become big companies.

If you or your employees believe there is an ethical issue with saying you are able to do certain things, *make sure it truly is an ethical issue.*

Do not confuse current capability with positioning for future capability.

Understand this strategy. It is critical for growth.

Something to think about.

Chapter 18.
DIBBS - The Labels Will Kill You

One of the most important activities when selling products to the Department of Defense is packing and labeling your shipments correctly.

Many companies that sell product to the Department of Defense use a system called DLA's Internet Bid Board System (DIBBS). DLA purchases billions of dollars every year on DIBBS - https://www.dibbs.bsm.dla.mil.

Side Note. There are other systems for commodity sales. They include GSA Advantage, FEDMALL, and others. But DIBBS is the 800 pound gorilla so I'll stick with it.

Before I discuss packaging and labeling, let me provide a couple of initial pointers. From a business development perspective, you need to learn the various strategies for searching and finding opportunities. DIBBS is a different system from SAM.

If you are new to DIBBS and you want to start searching today, I would recommend *not focusing* on national stock numbers (NSN) or federal supply codes. You will eventually want to use these but there is an easier method for companies that are new to DIBBS. Focus on Commercial and Government Entity (CAGE) codes *for your manufacturers and distributors*. If you know all your NSNs, great! Use them! If not, focusing on CAGE codes will show you each opportunity that is for a product carried by your manufacturers (or distributors).

Finding opportunities, knowing how to competitively bid on them and understanding how to read a DIBBS solicitation can be time consuming. You can master it in a matter of weeks or months. Completing a bid on an opportunity can be done in a matter of minutes.

What takes time is understanding how to be competitive.

You have to learn how to apply for and how to use the systems where you find diagrams, documentation on military specifications, and product specifications. You also have to learn the tactics and strategies on how to *consistently* be competitive.

If you need help with DIBBS, both finding opportunities and bidding on them, there are several resources you should use:

- The Defense Logistics Agency (DLA) has several outstanding guides on their websites.

- I have referred to the Federal Access Knowledge-Base and Training Platform (https://rsmfederal.com/FA) in several chapters. There are step-by-step guides for tactically and strategically responding to DIBBS opportunities. These resources include a step-by-step walkthrough, with graphics, screen-captures, techniques, and strategies to get you up and running.

Okay. Let's discuss packaging and labeling. Understanding the codes for packing, labeling, and shipping is one of the **most challenging issues** that companies face. In fact, there are companies that provide software (paid services) to help you identify how an order needs to be packed, labeled, and shipped.

There are so many different code combinations it will make your head spin. You cannot simply pack your product in a box and take it to the post office. The RFQ may require that every item be labeled and in its own bag. However, you may get your product from the manufacturer with 25 units per bag. Did you ship with 25 to a bag because it was easier or did you separate, bag each one, *and label each bag*?

If your shipment requires a pallet, is the pallet labeled correctly? Not the products, the pallet. Does the RFQ require a radio frequency identification (RFID) tag? You will have to have some of these on hand. Don't let 'RFID" scare you. Technology has come a long way and RFID tags now look like those name tags you put on your shirt at networking events.

Side note. I've helped several companies identify the software, tags, and hardware required to do this correctly. On average, you're looking at around $10,000 for all the pieces. You don't need this to start on DIBBS but when you start winning a bunch of contracts and you're shipping weekly, you'll quickly recognize the value.

Depending on the size of your shipment and the number of products being shipped, you might get away with the wrong labels. But don't bet on it.

When you ship a product to the government, many of these shipments are received at warehouses that look like the warehouse in the movie Raiders of the Lost Ark.

When shipments are received, they are quickly accepted or thrown into the 'problem area.' If all you shipped was one product in one box, you may get away with some labeling issues. But if the shipment is 500 items and the packing / labeling / shipping codes require each product to have a label, it is immediately obvious if the 500 items in the box do not have labels.

When this happens, the order is thrown into the corner of the warehouse. When you check the status in the Wide Area Work Flow (WAWF) system, it will say *"Price or Quantity Discrepancy."* After you win a DIBBS contract, it is automatically entered into WAWF, an online system. This is also where you update that the product has shipped, where the government accepts your shipment, and where you invoice it. The system does much more than this but those are some of the basics.

When your shipment is thrown into the problem area, it is going to be *very hard for anyone to find it.* The 'problem area' may be a dark corner of the warehouse.

If your shipment goes into a dark corner, this may explain why it can take months for you to figure out why you haven't been paid. You keep emailing and calling the government. They confirm the shipment was received but cannot explain why the end-user has not accepted it. Then it can take weeks or months for the end-user to find the shipment (in the problem area) and finally get back to the contracting officer.

Here is a real-world example that I saw a few months ago. A company shipped 2,000 tools to a military base that was re-outfitting their maintenance teams. Each type of tool had to be in separate boxes. Some tools had to be bagged in units of one and others in units of ten or twenty.

When the two pallets arrived at the warehouse, all of the tools had been packed in the original bags sent by the manufacturer. The manufacturer, by default, ships 100 units per bag. In order for the military to keep track of these tools and to assign them to their users, the tools had to be properly packaged. They were not.

143

If you are thinking, "Oh come on! They could just pull them out and put them in piles," you would be wrong. Since they were not packaged correctly, there were not enough bar codes to properly issue and track them. It would take someone in the warehouse somewhere between two and four hours to run labels on a computer, use their own bags (which they paid for - not you), and then physically repackage.

Now imagine what happens if the warehouse receives ten of these mis-labeled shipments every day! This is what happens, right now, at many government locations. This is why packaging and labeling is so important.

For the company that experienced this issue, it took the government **four months** to find the shipment and explain the problem to the contractor.

The contracting officer finally called them and said, "I'm sorry, but you did not follow the packaging and labeling instructions for the products you shipped. You have two options. You can either pay us to properly pack and label your products or you can ship the pallets back to your warehouse, fix it yourself, and send it back to us.

Oh. My. God. Remember, this happened just a couple months ago. The cost for the government to repack and label the items would be $3,500. The government would subtract this from the invoice. For this company, *this was their entire profit*. They would break-even at best.

The second option of shipping it back was unfathomable. First, they would have to find a local company to pick it up. The cost of shipping two more times, back to the contractor's warehouse and then back to the government, far exceeded the $3,500 cost to have the government do it. We are talking around $8,000.

If this was a $100,000 order, that is $100,000 of product / cash-flow tied up for four to six months!

In this real-world example, you only have two options. Break-even with no profit or take a loss. The company paid the government to repack and relabel the shipment.

Of course, there is always an upside. If you fail to properly pack and label a large shipment, you will quickly learn to never do it wrong again.

Yes, you can use the Vendor Shipment Module (VSM) to print your labels. This is a free application provided by DLA. In my opinion, it is not much help in translating the packaging, labeling, and shipping codes in the RFQ.

There are several third-party solutions that companies use to quickly identify their packaging and labeling requirements. Yes, they cost money. You can find a good one for $1,000 a year. (This is part of that $10,000 cost I referred to earlier). I highly recommend these third-party systems. Mess up two or three shipments and you will be paying much more than $1,000. Need some recommendations? Contact your local Procurement Technical Assistance Center (PTAC). While they are not authorized to recommend specific companies, they can help direct you in your search.

There is much more to DIBBS than what I have covered on the fulfillment side. I wanted to make sure you understood the danger of not correctly packaging and labeling your orders. If you are serious about selling through DIBBS, you should consider a third-party packing and labeling software solution to augment your team in the warehouse. It is worth every penny.

DIBBS looks easy. It can be if you understand how the system works.

This chapter provides a cautionary tale for companies new to DIBBS contracts.

Tens of thousands of companies make a living by selling on DIBBS. I want to make sure that companies, especially small businesses, understand that packaging and labeling should not be a secondary focus.

Something to think about.

Chapter 19.
Your Contract Is Protested
Don't Sit Back!

Y ou win a new contract. You are super-excited and with good reason. But then the wind is taken out of your sales when the contracting officer calls and says you cannot start work or ship the product because *your award* is being protested.

Most companies hang their head and fail to take action. Many companies think, "Damn! We know the protesting company has no legs to stand on. I wonder how many days or weeks it will take for the protest to be denied?"

Most companies simply wait for the contracting officer or the Government Accountability Office (GAO) to make a decision.

But here is the problem. You cannot assume that the agency or GAO is interested in defending *your* award. I am not implying that they are not going to follow the laws and regulations. But they do not know you or your company. They likely do not know the company that lodged the protest.

If the company that protested is quoting regulations or they have an email from the contracting officer that implies some dubious advantage during the acquisition, the contracting officer or GAO may simply say, "Yep, looks like there is questionable doubt on this. Cancel the contract and recompete it (or recommend giving it to the company that came in second place). There are quite a few options that can take place. *All but one option is bad for you!*

There are three ways for a company to protest your award; directly with the contracting officer (the most common), with GAO, and with the Court of Federal Claims. Protesting with one does not prevent later protesting with another. In many cases, companies that understand their rights and how protests work do not need a lawyer for protests with the agency or GAO.

For protests, the majority are handled through the agency. The GAO is the second most common. Considering the total number of protests, very few make it to the Court of Federal Claims.

Do you need a lawyer if you are filing a protest? It depends on how you are protesting. You probably do not need one for the agency. You should consider one for GAO. You must absolutely have a lawyer for the Court of Federal Claims.

Do you need a lawyer if you are *defending against a protest* and trying to protect your award? The answer depends on the value of the contract, its strategic value to your company, and whether it is the contracting officer or GAO. If you won an award and you get a letter saying, "Take no further action. Your contract is under protest," whether or not you need a lawyer depends, to some extent, on the value of the contract. On the other hand, if you have been working six months to win your first contract with a specific agency, then the value of the contract may be immaterial!

If you win a multi-million-dollar award and you are at risk of losing it to a protest, you should seriously consider getting an attorney that specializes in government acquisition and protests. I know several excellent attorneys that specialize in supporting *small and large businesses*. For a multitude of reasons, I will not list them here. But if you find yourself in this situation, contact me at contact@rsmfederal.com and I will make an introduction.

Regardless of the value of the contract, you *always* respond back to the contracting officer telling them you want to know on what grounds it is being protested. Do not be passive. Do not allow the protest to take place without injecting yourself into the process. If the contracting officer tells you there is nothing you can do, you are still going to inject yourself. An exception is if you are going to retain an attorney. If you are getting an attorney, then hold off and follow your attorney's guidance.

When the contracting officer tells you why it is being protested, respond back with documentation, proof, everything the contracting officer needs to deny the protest. Be proactive. I used this quote earlier in the book: "Hope is not a strategy." Do you really want to hang that multi-million-dollar contract on... hope?

Protests can be defended (you keep the award), upheld (you lose the contract), or the contracting office cancels the contract and restarts the entire procurement process (again, you lose the contract and have to bid on it again). There can also be variations of these three.

Over the last year, there were *tens of thousands of protests* made through agency contracting offices and through the Small Business Administration (SBA). Many protests are based on affiliation, business size, or socio-economic status. There are thousands of protests for product procurements that could be for as little as several hundred dollars.

Specific to GAO, in the previous twelve months, there were 2,621 protests. An interesting fact is that 375 protests were for task orders, about 14% of GAO protests. The GAO reviews task order protests if the task order exceeds $10M.

The GAO sustained 22% of protests. That means that one out of every five contract awards were successfully protested in some manner.

Think about that. 22% of protests were upheld by the GAO. That means if you win a large contract and it gets protested with the GAO, you have a 22% chance of *losing* your contract.

Do you still want to sit back, like most companies, and hope that the protest is denied? Do you really like those odds?

So, what should you do? First, you *always defend* your contract award. You defend awards that are a million dollars. You defend awards that are $150.

Government employees are a microcosm of society. They are busy. They have other priorities. They may be too busy to research and they may not have any desire to defend your award. They also make mistakes. Do not sit back and simply wait. You need to be proactive. You need to defend your contract award. Many companies that protest are hoping that you will do nothing. Do not make it easy for them to take your money.

Something else to consider. When a company protests your award, they may ask for certain information you do not want them to see. Though not common, it is possible for some of your documentation to become public.

You need to protect yourself. I always recommend that our clients and Federal Access members put 'business sensitive' on *every* document that leaves the office. I also recommend that your proposal and all other documentation include a confidentiality paragraph on the title page that says, "all information is business sensitive and none of the information should be made public or disclosed to other parties without asking you first." This not only protects you during a protest, but also in the event another company files a freedom of information act (FOIA) request.

Copies of your proposal, your pricing, and proprietary information should never be released. But I have seen it happen on quite a few occasions. The contracting officer is not thinking clearly, does not see business sensitive or confidential, and accidentally releases your information.

Most contracting officers and FOIA offices normally ask you to review your documentation first. You get to blackline everything you believe is business sensitive. This has happened to my company several times. By the time I was done blacklining the document, the only words you could read were pronouns, conjunctions, and prepositions. I blacklined 99% of the document. It looked like one of those publicly released intelligence reports on Area 51 and UFOs. My five-year-old could read what was left. The contracting officer did not say anything when I gave it back to him. He knows how the game is played.

Put business sensitive on *everything* that leaves your office.

Now, the next point is controversial. There is an entire industry of law firms and lawyers that specialize in government contracting. I have relationships with several of the top government law firms in the nation. I refer clients to them. I speak at conferences and sit on panels with these attorneys. They are my friends and colleagues. They have been guests on our Podcast Game Changers for Government Contractors (iTunes and Soundcloud). Their services are essential... when you need them. However, I do not believe that **small businesses** need them on full-time retainer. (OMG - they are yelling at me right now).

Many of them say, "A legal review should be a part of your corporate sales and proposal strategy." What they are saying is that you should have an attorney reviewing every proposal that you write.

Yes! They will protect your interests. The problem with this is that a fairly large number of smaller businesses cannot afford to keep an attorney on retainer to review the acquisition strategy and proposal for each and every opportunity.

If you have been in the market for several years and understand how protests work, you probably do not need an attorney for agency level and some GAO level protests.

Just last year, one of our Federal Access members called and said that their $6 million award was under protest. The contracting officer implied that it would likely not end in their favor. I immediately connected them with a colleague, a well-known small business attorney and yes, it cost about $15,000 over four months. However, they successfully defended the protest. $15,000 versus a $6 million contract. There is always risk in business. But you also have to *see the forest through the trees (another one of my favorite quotes)*.

I am not an attorney (and I can still hear the attorneys screeching at me) but I simply want to point out that how you decide to engage attorneys, for protests, is simply a question of ***identifying your level of risk***. Just because you know how to submit a protest does not mean you know how to defend against one. You have to identify your level of acceptable risk. How much is the opportunity worth to you?

So, what should you do when your award is protested? Whether agency or GAO, send a letter demonstrating you are an interested party (that you were involved in the acquisition process) and that you are intervening. You need to explain why the protested issue is not viable and why the contract should be upheld.

There is no formal format for agency or GAO protests and no formal format for you to respond back for defending your award. If you have to defend one of your contracts, cannot afford an attorney, and you need a template, go to the Federal Access Knowledge-Base (https://rsmfederal.com/FA). There is a dynamite on-demand webinar called "When and How to Protest."

I have been in the government market for more than 30 years and I understand the core strategies involved in both protesting and defending against a protest. I've provided advice and recommendations to several hundred companies that has protected over $100 million. For a good number of them, yes, I have had to refer them to a small business attorney.

Bottom line, do not sit back when your contract is protested. Be proactive. How proactive and whether or not you engage an attorney is based on contract value, what you can afford, the strategic value of the contract, and at what level the protest is made.

Something to think about.

Chapter 20.
Scams and Pitfalls – Those Blood-Suckers

W ithin 24 hours of registering in the System for Award Management (SAM), you started receiving emails from companies that want your money. Some offer solid value. Some offer snake oil.

I want to discuss companies that target you and your company and promise millions of dollars in contracts. Many provide little value. Some outright lie. *They prey on the less educated.*

As I tell our clients and members, everything you do in your company comes down to two and only two outcomes. You are either increasing revenue or you are decreasing costs. I am going to discuss a couple of ways of doing both.

I am going to run down a list of seven scams that should raise red flags when you receive an email or phone call with a pitch for government support. Some of these are outright scams and others are *just bad business decisions*. While I only list seven of them, there are twenty or thirty variations. *I am not saying these are illegal*. I am saying they are *bad business decisions*.

I have discussed these various times over the years and I often receive hate-mail from the companies that provide these services. So, if you are one of these companies, feel free to write and explain why companies should waste their money on your services. I will continue educating companies on why your services are bad business decisions. Not that I have an opinion.

Number 1.
Help you with registrations

You should already know that registering for your DUNS / SAMMI number and your profile in System for Award Management (SAM) is free. But there are companies that put a different spin on this and imply that your SAM registration is incomplete. Other than perhaps your NAICS and PSC codes or accepting credit cards, your registration is either accepted or it is not. I really detest companies that prey on small businesses new to the market.

There are also con-artists that will charge you $500 to $1,500 a year to 'manage' your SAM account. There is absolutely no possible reason why you should ever consider this! If you have to update a NAICS code, just login and do it. If you need to do your annual renewal, spend fifteen minutes verifying your information and click submit. If you are having issues, call the federal help desk or go to your local procurement technical assistance center (PTAC) and they will help you for free.

These con-artists use persuasive arguments. They say, *"Some companies just don't have the time and we help them manage their accounts and ensure that there are never any issues. Some companies simply prefer to outsource it."*

Every single company I have spoken to that has paid for this has turned-around and said, "You don't need to outsource this! I wasted a lot of money because the process was mysterious to me. If I had simply done it myself, I would have figured it out pretty fast."

In general, any email or phone call you get about DUNS / SAMMI, SAM, or any other system being incomplete is just someone trying to empty your pockets.

Similarly, I often get asked about certifications. For full transparency, my company, RSM Federal, provides certification support as a boutique service. These services include GSA Schedule application services and socio-economic certification services (8a, VOSB, SDVOSB, and HUBZone). **We always recommend that our clients first attempt to do it on their own.** Look at our website or attend any of my keynotes or seminars. I make crystal clear that companies should always attempt to do it on their own. Then if they need help, they know who to call.

Even if you are still on the fence about paying for SAM support, go look at the APTAC's website! This is the federally funded organization for helping small businesses get started in government sales. The first thing they tell you on the website's homepage is that registering and maintaining your SAM account is free. The government is telling you it's free.

Number 2.
Incomplete DUNS Listing

If you get a call from any company that wants to help you with improving your DUNS number listing, just hang up. Dun and Bradstreet provides a very important service.

They provide you with a *free* DUNS number in order to register with the Government. Once you have your DUNS number, you will not hear from them again. But there are some companies that harass small businesses with unethical scare tactics. They tell you that several companies have 'accessed your profile' and due to an incomplete profile, you are losing business. Do not fall for it.

Earlier in the book I mentioned that Ernst & Young LLP is taking over the unique identifier program after several decades with Dun and Bradstreet. I believe one of the reasons for the government taking the contract away from Dun and Bradstreet is that the government wants to control, manage, and own the numbers. From a business perspective, it makes perfect sense. Hence, one reason the contract was competed in 2019 and awarded to Ernst & Young.

So until the new SAMMI number replaces the DUNS number, watch-out for companies that say you have an incomplete profile and you're losing contracts.

Ever heard of ripoffreport.com? Look these companies up. Do not waste hundreds or thousands of dollars.

Bottom line, do not pay for SAM. Do not pay for Dun and Bradstreet (DUNS). Do not pay for updating the Small Business Dynamic Search (SBDS) which you create / update during your SAM registration.

Number 3.
Paying for Teaming Services

I do not want to take away from some very good consultants and management consulting firms that provide this as a *supporting service*, but do not pay money to simply find and team with other companies. No matter how strong they market the service, knowing who to talk to is one thing. Knowing what to say and how to position with other companies is entirely different.

If it is a free service, go ahead. The company is more than likely trying to get you to pay for other services. There is nothing wrong with them trying to upsell another service. My company provides various free products to introduce companies to other valuable services we provide. Most companies do it. LinkedIn does it. Amazon does it. But if you want to know who to team with, search the Federal Procurement Data System (FPDS) / SAM; join your industry's association; go to conferences. But do not spend money to simply join a "teaming network."

Learning where to find companies to team with is easy! You just have to know where to go. So, if you are looking for teaming partners:

- USASpending.gov

- Federal Procurement Data System (FPDS) / SAM NOTE [22]

- GSA eLibrary (companies that have GSA Schedules and sell what you sell)

- Call that agency's small business office and ask for recommendations

- Attend government conferences for your industry

- Attend industry days for various opportunities

Number 4.
Your SAP Registration Is Incomplete

In Chapter 11, we discussed Simplified Acquisition Procedures (SAP). *There is no government registration for accessing SAP opportunities*! If you find a website for registration, it will not have a .gov or .mil domain. SAP is an acquisition decision made at the contracting office level. Do not fall for this. My company is in SAM and we get two of these emails every month. I know better. I often wonder how many companies fall for this scam. It is depressing to think of how many entrepreneurs and small business owners are impacted. Another reason for writing this book.

---

[22] FPDS is migrating into the Integrated Award Environment (IAE) and will be part of System for Award Management (SAM) in 2020.

Number 5.
Business Offers From Generic Domains

An email that comes from Hotmail, Gmail, Yahoo, or similar email account is a red-flag. Just because emails come from professional looking domains does not guarantee it is a legitimate company or service. But if you pay money to a company with a Gmail account, you are unlikely to get what you paid for. Is this 100% accurate? Of course not. There are always exceptions. But why gamble? If it is a reputable business, why do they not have a professional company domain? By all means accept the risk if you have done your due diligence. If you do decide to engage one of these companies, make sure that you get no less than three referrals and *call every single one.*

Number 6.
Paying For List of Buyers

If you have an account in the System for Award Management (SAM) you have probably received emails asking you to pay for a list of government buyers that buy what you sell. It does not matter how much data or information you get, this is *free information*! I received an email last week from a company that wants to sell me the top 250 buyers for what I sell. Is this information important? *Absolutely.* But I can find that information for free, in ten minutes, using FPDS / SAM or USASpending.gov.

These companies send out 100,000 emails and hope that 50 uneducated businesses pay for it. I find charging for free data to be highly unethical. Some disagree with me. Just call me old-fashioned.

If you do not know who buys what you sell, how much they buy, and how often they buy it, you want to start with your local PTAC. It's free. Other resources include my company's resources www.rsmfederal.com.

Number 7.
Hail-Mary Teaming Opportunities

"Dear Mr. Frank! There is a major Indefinite Delivery Indefinite Quantity (IDIQ) contract, worth $20 Billion, and 10 teams will be selected. If you want to be a part of this, we are putting a team together – Call Now!"

First, you almost always receive these emails *after* the RFP has been released. The teams that are going to be competitive *have already built their teams and written a draft proposal*. They started six months ago. 90% of the time, if you join a team for a large opportunity after the RFP has been released AND the Prime did not know about the opportunity until after the RFP was released, *that team has little chance of winning*.

No absolutes on this one. If you have no other choice, sure, go ahead and join that team. However, instead of joining that team, I would recommend that you focus on other opportunities in your pipeline. If you can get on a team with little impact to your internal activities, sure, sign a teaming agreement (TA). You have nothing to lose. But even if the team wins, you are not likely to get a lot of work. Always try to join a team and sign a teaming agreement *before* the final RFP is released.

Getting an email "out of the blue" by some company you have never heard of - that invites you to be on their team... think about it! You don't know them. They don't know you. They sent that email to every veteran business or 8a business or woman-owned small business that was listed in the System for Award Management (SAM). You and how many other companies will be on this team? Eight-five?

Some of these teams actually win now and then. But very few actually win task orders or make money. If you have no other options, go for it. But set realistic expectations.

In summary, there is a reason all of these companies exist. All companies market and position with their prospects. As such, not all emails you receive are cons or scams. But many of them would be a bad business decision.

My number one recommendation? Find someone like myself that understands the government market and ask them what they think of the offer you just received. It can potentially save you thousands of dollars.

Something to think about.

Chapter 21.
Why Are You Still Teaming with Them?

Y ou know that company you team with all the time? You know, the one you met at that conference two years ago? Why are you still teaming with them? In this chapter, I want you to think about the companies you have been teaming with.

What is the definition of insanity? *"It is doing the same thing over and over again and expecting different results."* We have all heard this phrase.

So, that one company you have been teaming with for the last two years? The one that you have teamed with half-a-dozen times and still have not won any contracts? At what point are you simply teaming with this company, over and over again, and expecting different results?

Let's pause for a minute. Seriously, why are you still teaming with them?

I mentioned a concept earlier in the book called the 'small business vortex'. It is where small businesses gravitate to building relationships and teaming with companies that have the *same or less level of corporate and / or market maturity*.

For example, the owner of a woman owned small business (WOSB) is much more likely to build relationships with other woman owned small businesses. Same goes for 8a. Same goes for most small companies.

For many business owners and business developers, you attend a conference and meet a business owner or business developer that is very eager to teach you what they have learned. They have been in your shoes. They have successfully won a prime government contract. Maybe they won two contracts. Many business developers and owners will latch-onto these folks.

You say, "This is awesome! They know what they are doing. They have past performance. They want to work and team with my company! A week later, they put you onto a team for an opportunity with the Department of Justice (DOJ).

It was really close but your team did not win. A month later, they put you on a team for an opportunity with the Army. Grrrrrrr – so close but your team lost again. This is very common. It is not unusual for companies to lose the first couple of bids. Over the next 12 months you partner with them on another four or five opportunities and you do not win a single one.

Now, during the last year, you have been crazy busy. You have been talking with several other companies. You have been in meetings with government prospects. You are on a couple other teams. You are also attending training events and conferences. You are doing a million different things.

But, are you keeping perspective? You have not only built a business relationship with this other company, but you have also become good friends. You are sharing your pipelines. You are doing business development together. However, that contract they won, before you met, was three years ago. It was their first or second contract.

This company is what I call a 'two-contract-wonder.' It is what I call companies that may have simply been lucky and are really no more mature than your company.

So, now you have built this extensive relationship with them. You have spent hundreds of labor hours bidding contracts with them. Even though you may not see it, they have little chance of winning. How do I know this? Because they have not won a new contract in three years. Because you have bid on contracts with them and they have never won as prime. You have never won with them on your team.

This is a symptom of the "small business vortex.' So, when you think about your teaming partners, ask yourself the following questions:

- Is this relationship generating revenue?

- With each teaming partner, how many proposals have you submitted and how many have you won?

- How long have you been working with this partner?

If you haven't won a contract with them and it has been more than 14 months, you need to ask yourself if it is time to change your strategy.

I am not recommending you cut them loose. You need to consciously make sure you are not spending a lot of time with them. You have proven, over time, that this relationship simply is not competitive enough to win contracts.

Yes, you should maintain the relationship. Every dog has its day. But you should start looking for other teaming partners.

The *vast* majority of companies' you team with should be *more mature than you* from a corporate, market, and government contracting perspective.

Do not fall into the vortex and gravitate towards companies that are just like yours; no matter how right it feels.

You want to make sure you are keeping your strategy in perspective.

Is it working? No? Then change it.

If you do not change it, you are doing the same thing over and over again... expecting different results.

Something to think about.

Chapter 22.
Failure to Team. Failure to Win.

L et's talk about how and when to engage multiple award contract (MAC) vehicles. Oftentimes, they are called indefinite delivery indefinite quantity (IDIQ) contracts. They may also be called single award task order contracts (SATOC), multiple award task order contracts (MATOC), or government wide acquisition contracts (GWAC). There are others.

There are many examples of large MACs where the ceiling value for these contracts range from the millions to billions of dollars. They are often 5 to 10-year contracts.

There are three core principles every company should know. First, whether you prime or subcontract, you almost always want to create a team or join a team. A team enables the prime to communicate stronger past performance and capability. A team normally makes a response more competitive.

Second, most teams are put together long before you see the opportunity on SAM. Trying to put together a team after the RFP is released will often make for a good proposal with the possibility of winning, but not a great proposal that gives you competitive advantage.

Third, and this is one of the most popular discussions we have with our clients. Many RFPs say you do not have to submit a response on every product, service, or task area group. The government says, "This acquisition is for six different task area groups (TAG). Contractors can bid on one or more."

I strongly recommend you only respond and write a proposal if you have past performance in every task area group. Yes, you will likely need to build a team.

Here is what happens. Dozens of companies see the RFP / RFQ on SAM. These companies are all capable of supporting one, two or three of the task area groups. It should be no surprise that many companies that respond to only several task areas are the same companies that heard about the opportunity *only after the RFP was released.*

Companies that spend several months building their teams almost always make sure that their team has strong capability and past performance in *every* task area. It is very important to understand this difference because it speaks directly to business strategy and competitive capability.

Every opportunity is different. Every MAC is different. Some allow you to only submit on one or two task areas. Others require that your proposal respond to every one.

Think about this. Put yourself in the shoes of source selection. For many of the large MACs there can be between 500 and several thousand responses. That's 500 to 1,000 proposals they have to review.

If 80% of the proposals successfully respond to every task area in the RFP and I am on source selection, I immediately recognize that it will be more advantageous if I select companies and teams that can support *all the requirements.*

For example, one hundred proposals will be down-selected (these have the strongest technical response). Will I be more likely to award a contract to a company that can only do 30% of future task orders or a company that I know can do 100% of future task orders?

To be accurate, yes, there are a good number of MACs where they award contracts to companies that only responded to several of the task areas.

But from a perspective of building competitive advantage; from your perspective, it is important that you *mitigate as much risk as possible.* You are spending time, money, and manpower to prime or subcontract. You need to put yourself in the most competitive position that you can.

So yes, you can respond, without a team, to a select number of task areas, but you have to recognize that your proposal may not be highly competitive if most of the other companies and teams are responding to all task areas.

So, what should you do if you find an opportunity for a large MAC on SAM and you are not on a team yet? If you have at least 30 days to respond, you can put a team together. If you only have a few weeks, your best bet is to find a team to join. Remember, most teams for these large MACs started working on the opportunity months or years before the final RFP was released.

How do you find a team? Contact the contracting officer and tell them that you would like a list of the companies that attended industry day so you can find a team to join.

If the contracting officer will not tell you, contact the small business office for that agency or military command.

Run a query on USASpending.gov or the federal procurement data system (FPDS) / SAM to find out which companies are currently managing contracts with that agency or military command. Call them and ask if they are going after the current opportunity.

The longer you are selling to the government, the easier it will be to engage and participate in these larger contracts. The longer you are in the government market, the more relationships you will have with other companies.

Are you going to respond to an RFP in only a couple of task areas or will you build or join a team to cover-down on all of them?

Are you mitigating your risk? *How competitive do you want to be?*

Something to think about.

Chapter 23.
Teaming Agreements Have No Teeth

I f you have been active in the government market for several months, you have probably heard of a Teaming Agreement (TA). If you are unfamiliar with this process, it works like this: two companies want to work together to win a contract. One is the prime contractor. The other is a subcontractor to the prime. A prime can have one or more subcontractors on the team. To seal the working relationship, the prime offers the subcontractor a teaming agreement.

Teaming agreements are *opportunity specific*. If two companies agree to work together throughout the year, they do not sign a teaming agreement. They sign some form of a partnership agreement. With or without a partnership agreement, *every* opportunity, where two companies bid together (one as prime and the other as a subcontractor), *should* sign a teaming agreement. Teaming agreements are signed between two companies *every time* they jointly go after an opportunity.

Yes, there are variations. They can include mentor-protégé (MP), joint ventures (JV), and contractor teaming arrangements (CTA) which are specific to two GSA Schedule holders. But even under these other relationships, there is still a managing company that has the lead on a given opportunity and contract.

So, to be clear, if you plan to prime an opportunity and you are going to build a team to be more competitive, then you should give a teaming agreement (TA) to each subcontractor that will be on your team.

If you plan to subcontract, you are not locked-in as a subcontractor to the prime until after the *prime* gives *you* a teaming agreement. *The prime is responsible for the teaming agreement process.*

Before we continue, I am going to go off on yet another tangent. Let's discuss non-disclosure agreements (NDA) versus teaming agreements (TA).

From experience, somewhere between 10% and 20% of companies use stand-alone NDAs to initiate business discussions with other companies. It is not required but some companies use NDAs as a standard process. When I was selling collaborative technology to the Department of Defense in the early 2000's, every company I contacted had to sign an NDA. It was a corporate policy. The owner felt that the NDA was a legal necessity. There is no right or wrong answer on the use of NDAs.

That being said, my company does not use them very often. Why? Because strong teaming agreements (TA) and partnership agreements have NDA language built into them. There is not a right or wrong process when it comes to using or not using separate NDAs. In the government market, many companies skip the NDA and go straight to teaming agreements. Every situation is different. Just recognize that many companies skip the NDA, have a quick call with the other company, and move straight into a teaming agreement.

To summarize, the process is teaming agreement (with an NDA built-in), followed by a subcontracting agreement (SubK), followed by contract execution.

Don't Rely On The Prime For Award Notification

Once the teaming agreement is signed, the two companies work together to collect intelligence. Companies collect market intelligence because the more information you have, the more competitive the team will be. The proposal will be more competitive.

Once the proposal or bid is turned-in, it moves to source selection and then award.

When the contract is awarded, the government notifies the prime. They do not notify the subcontractors. As a subcontractor, you are not an *interested party*. You did not respond to the acquisition. The prime did. You are just along for the ride.

This means you have to keep your eyes open and your ears to the ground. I often tell our clients to create a query in SAM or in their bid-matching tool to specifically track the opportunity. This way, regardless of the Prime contacting you, you will know that the team you are on won the contract.

Speaking of being an interested party, allow me to go down the rabbit hole on one other item. If you're not the prime, the government is not going to notify you of... anything. You're not an interested party.

I've seen this done by several companies and considered by others. Let's say the team lost the bid. You and several other subcontractors swear up and down that it was unfair and should be protested, but your prime has no desire to protest (for whatever reason). These companies are mad and attempt to circumvent the prime and try to protest directly with the government. It NEVER works. These subcontractors are not interested parties. To be an interested party, you must have submitted a proposal or bid to the government. The government won't even look at your reasons.

Several times I have seen a prime win a contract and fail to notify some of their team members. Why? Because they are unethical. Sometimes they want to negotiate better pricing with other companies to increase their margins. It happens. It is not a rampant issue, but it does happen. So, do not rely on the prime to notify you of award. Make sure you are watching for the award online. You can also email the contracting officer and ask for an update.

99% of the time you *will* receive an email or call from the prime saying they won the award. When you get that call, celebrate and then work with the prime to get your share of the work.

Negotiating In Good Faith

There is another lesson on teaming agreements that is the core of this chapter. Once the prime is awarded the contract, the next step is 'negotiating' subcontracts with each of their subcontractors. You may be thinking, "Why am I negotiating anything? I'm on the team. I helped with the proposal. I have a teaming agreement."

For those new to government contracting, most teaming agreements have two important clauses. One is for exclusivity. The other says, "When the prime is notified by the government of award, the prime will *negotiate in good faith* with each subcontractor for work on the contract."

The phrase 'negotiate in good faith' is very important. This gives the prime all the legal justification it needs to say, "We tried negotiating with you, in good faith, but we could not come to an agreement."

In other words, *you are no longer on the team.*

Yes, I have seen this dozens of times.

This can happen for various reasons. As discussed previously, the prime may want to increase their margins and mandates that you lower your pricing. Is it ethical? No, but until you have a signed subcontracting agreement (SubK), *the prime holds all the cards.*

Even if you provided your pricing during the proposal / bid phase, the prime **can still renegotiate your pricing as part of the subcontracting agreement**. The prime can legally demand new pricing. It happens, at some level, on many, many contracts.

Perhaps the prime screwed-up in their overall pricing. They won but they still have no choice but to require that all subcontractors drop their pricing by three or five points.

You might be thinking, "Hey! That is not my problem!"

Well, yes, it is. The prime may not have intentionally mis-priced their bid. The "negotiate in good faith" clause allows them to not only get better pricing whenever they want, but to also rectify their own pricing mistakes. Your company would not accept a contract for a loss. Why would you expect a prime you work for to do the same? It may have been an honest mistake.

Consider the following real-world example. During the teaming and proposal phase you were promised four of nine positions on a contract. When the contract is awarded, the prime negotiates a subcontract for only two positions. You are angry and rightfully so. But the prime holds all the cards. In this example, yes, this is unethical, but it is still legal.

But what if you had a strong teaming agreement that guaranteed you those four positions? You may be thinking, "Wait! I had those four positions listed in the teaming agreement! We have a signed agreement!" You would be correct. But the clause in the teaming agreement for 'negotiating in good faith' provides the prime contractor with the authority and justification to renegotiate with you.

There are no absolutes. I am simply outlining some situations and practices you may experience in the government market.

A *teaming agreement has no teeth*. Yes, all government contractors use teaming agreements as part of their business development and capture strategy. However, they provide minimal legal protection to subcontractors. They favor the prime.

Teaming agreements are less enforceable than you would like. Teaming agreements are written to provide maximum advantage to the *prime contractor*.

It does not mean that you should not use them. *You absolutely should use them*. But you need to understand that a teaming agreement, **without a strong relationship**, is nothing more than a piece of paper.

In fact, I would never assume you are on a team (where you are subcontracting to a prime contractor) unless you have a signed teaming agreement. I cannot overemphasize the importance of this point. If the prime says, "Sure, you are on the team," your immediate response is, "Excellent. If you will forward a teaming agreement, I will get it signed and returned in the next day or two."

If the prime says, "Oh, we don't use teaming agreements" or "There is no need for a teaming agreement," *those are major red-flags*. You are either on the team or you are not.

If you do not have a teaming agreement, *you are not on the team*.

I have provided several cautionary tales. But if you want to win government contracts, you want a teaming agreement every time you engage with another company.

I do not want you to think that this happens often. Most companies honor their teaming agreements. But you should be aware of these issues so that you can properly mitigate them when they occur.

Something to think about.

Chapter 24.
The Prime Stole Our Work!

T his chapter is about prime contractors that take advantage of their subcontractors. I'm talking about a prime winning a contract and then throwing you to the curb.

I wish this did not happen. But wishing and hoping are a recipe for failure. Unfortunately, a prime contractor stealing work from their subcontractors happens now and then. Every time I give a seminar, at least a couple of folks raise their hand when I ask if this has happened to them.

If this ever happens to you, I am going to provide you with a very strong strategy that will help protect your business position with the prime. I am going to show you how to get the prime to reverse their decision.

Some companies take advantage of other companies. It is a sometimes-unfortunate aspect of business. You get a call from another company and they say, "we would like you to be on our team." You sign a teaming agreement. The teaming agreement has the standard clause, "on award of contract, we will negotiate in good faith to sign a subcontracting agreement."

The proposal is submitted. Your team wins… and the prime does not call you. It takes two phone calls and three emails to learn that the prime is going to take all the work.

Most small companies do not know what to do. Most get angry, send a couple of overly emotional emails, swear to never work with that company again, and then they move on.

Again, over the life of your company, this does not happen that often. But it happens enough that I want to arm you with a strategy. I am going to give you a successful and very professional strategy to not only deal with this situation - but to get some of the work that you were promised.

Let's outline a real-world example that happened recently to a company I work with. We will start with the proposal. The proposal may or may not require a subcontracting plan. Regardless, the prime will normally use your company's name in the proposal. It makes sense. You are one of their subcontractors. You are a member of the team. You provided credibility to the response and your past performance made the team more competitive.

Going off on a tangent, did you know that a government contract in excess of $700,000 is required by the Federal Acquisition Regulation (FAR) to have a small business subcontracting plan? This means that the prime is required, by regulation, to include the small businesses, by name, in the proposal, that they will be using for subcontracting. Keep this in mind because if the value of the contract exceeds $700,000, you can be fairly certain that your company was listed in the proposal.

Regardless of the contract value, some primes will use one or two of your past performances (your past commercial and federal contracts) to communicate value and to create a more competitive response.

The proposal is submitted and the government moves into source selection. Then to the excitement of everyone on the team - you win. You are already envisioning what you will do with the money. You are planning your next hire. You are thinking about those fruity drinks with little umbrellas in the Cayman Islands.

It is a fact of life - not all companies are ethical. Sometimes, a company that you have a great relationship with may act in an unethical or unprofessional manner. Sometimes it is a company you have a great relationship with and have known for years.

You know the prime won the contract. You know that the award was due, in part, to the intelligence you gave them, your past performance, your help writing the proposal, or a combination.

When you finally get the prime on the phone, they say, "we are really sorry, but we are not going to be able to give you those positions on this contract" or "we are going to buy the product from someone else."

You go from being confused, to being stunned, to angry, to where you cannot breathe and fire is shooting out of your eyes.

Many small companies start screaming, "We had a deal! We have a teaming agreement! You can't do this!"

The prime responds, "I know, but some things have changed that are outside our control. I'm really sorry about this. But don't worry, we'll get you a position on the next contract we win."

At this point, you are mentally devising ways of delivering a thermonuclear detonation. It is understandable.

But let's take a step back. All is not lost. First, it is likely the prime is having cash-flow issues. They are either having trouble paying bills or they are just pure greedy and unethical. But regardless of the reason, *their problems are not your problems*. You spent time, money, and manpower supporting the primes efforts and proposal development. You should rightfully obtain what is due to you.

Do you really think they will give you a position on their next contract or purchase product through you? Of course not.

It is at this point that most small companies say, "there is nothing more we can do." You may think, "This is a mid-size or larger company and there are other opportunities we are trying to engage with them. We have no choice but to suck-in our pride and move on."

And that is almost always a mistake.

This is where you have to remind yourself that business is business. The size of your company or that of your teaming partner is immaterial. You would not do this to another company. Why? Because it is unethical and unprofessional. Whether you are a small or large company, you need to operate as an ethnical organization. If you do not, you will end up losing future business and no one will want to work with you. At the end of the day, all we have is our integrity. You would not let a company smaller than you to get away with this. Why would you allow a larger company to do it?

So, what can you do?

I am going to discuss a strategy that often forces a prime to give you some of the work that was agreed to. *Something is better than nothing.*

When done correctly, you come across as being highly professional with a *very astute understanding of government acquisition and procurement.*

Here is what you do:

You call the prime and after they say they are sorry they cannot give you work, you say the following:

"Tom, we both know that what you are doing is unfair, unethical, and unprofessional. Regardless of why you are doing this, we both know we have a signed teaming agreement. We both know that being on the team, being listed in the proposal, using our past performance, and helping you write a winning proposal is one of the key reasons why you won the contract. If you do not honor our agreement, you will be forcing me to escalate this to the government and I do not want to do that."

Okay, let's step back for a moment. You may already do this. But this is as far as many companies take it. They do not explain *how they will escalate*. Many small companies call the contracting officer and yes, this is something you should do. But the contracting officer does not want the headache.

Even with the new FAR regulations to protect small businesses that are on teams, you do not want to escalate to the government. *You want the prime to change its decision.* This is very important. This strategy is not about escalating to the government. It is about the prime's fear that you will.

Once you say, "you are forcing me to escalate this to the government," the prime often says, "Well, you do what you need to do."

But now you are going to do something that is politically very astute. You say:

"Tom, I don't think you understand. If we can't make this right, I am going to escalate per acquisition and FAR regulations."

"First, we are going to lodge a formal complaint with the contracting officer. I am going to explain we have a teaming agreement, the extent to which we helped you develop the proposal, your use of our company and past performance in the proposal (whether directly or indirectly referenced), and then how you took our work."

"Second, we will file a formal complaint with the director of the contracting division for the agency to ensure the contracting officer does not sweep this under the rug."

"Third, we will contact the SBA and ask them to investigate."

That's it. It is that simple. If the prime still does not change course, you are going to give them a black-eye. Most companies, most primes, will reconsider giving you the work. They *do not want to have their name dragged through the mud*, not when it could impact current or future contract opportunities. They do not want the three or four future RFPs with that agency to be impacted by this.

If you follow this strategy in a professional and *unemotional* manner, instead of screaming at them and walking away with nothing, you are likely to walk away with a part of the contract.

If you are thinking, "they will never work with us again!" You are absolutely right. But they just tried to screw you. It is unlikely you would work with them again. So, get everything that you can!

This isn't theoretical. I have provided this strategy to nine companies over the last several years. It worked eight times.

Be professional.

Do not get emotional.

Know your options.

Have a strategy.

Something to think about.

Chapter 25.
A Prime Demanding Out-of-Scope Work

This chapter is the about another major challenge that small businesses face when subcontracting. Whether the prime is a small or large business, the challenge of dealing with out-of-scope work is fairly universal. It is market agnostic. It happens in both commercial and government markets.

It can be unplanned meetings with the government, specifications for a product, or additional services you did not agree to. We are talking about anything that costs you money.

Every time you spend money, you are losing margin and profit. So, before we discuss how to deal with these, let's outline a few examples.

This one is very common. You have seven (7) full time employees (FTE) on a subcontract and the prime wants you or your manager to be physically present at monthly client meetings. Sounds like a common and smart business requirement.

But monthly onsite meetings *were not in the scope*. The agency's office is on the East coast and your office is on the West coast. The prime never mentioned this requirement during the proposal and pricing phase. You sure didn't estimate travel when you provided your pricing to the prime.

The prime wants you or someone on your management team to travel across the country, every month, for meetings with the government. Two of your seven FTEs are at the client's location. The other five employees work out of your office on the West coast and your team leader is at your West coast office.

Still, they want your senior employee, the team leader, or a manager to attend these meetings.

The prime may try to convince you that it is in your best interests. They may say:

*"There is follow-on work... or we know of another opportunity with the same agency and we need to put our best foot forward. It is in **your best interests** to have your team leader attend every month for the onsite meeting."*

No, it is not in your best interest. It is in the prime's best interest. That's $700 for airfare, lodging and travel... every month. That's $8,000 the prime wants you to eat.

They give you a very strong business case. They do not mention costs. They simply assume that since you are the subcontractor that you will fly someone up every month. They want you to think it is simply the 'price of doing business.'

It is not. It is scope-creep. If the prime wanted you to be there in person every month, they should have told you. You would have priced it into your numbers. They may be local to the government client but you are not. You simply assumed you would be calling-in via conference call.

This is a situation where the prime screwed-up and they do not want to ask the government for a contract modification or they do not want to 'eat it' and pay for your travel.

But let's take a step back. There is a flip-side to this discussion. If your team leader is very smart and you trust them with business development activities, you may want to consider eating that $8,000. If your team leader is not mature enough, perhaps you or the owner of the company should attend. (Just have the team leader attend by phone.)

Think about this for a minute. Your seven FTEs are supporting the Department of Labor (DOL). The only contract you have with DOL are these seven FTEs where you are subcontracting to another company. You want a prime contract with DOL but you need information, intelligence, and relationships.

What better way to collect intelligence and meet buyers and decision makers than to be onsite! You do not have to worry about a visitor access badge. The prime took care of it.

A week before one of these monthly meetings, you call several other offices that you have been trying to engage and say:

"Hi, this is Julie. I have a meeting with Mike in your building next Thursday. I wanted to swing by for five minutes that afternoon. Do you have time for a quick drive-by?"

Bam! It is so much easier meeting with new buyers and decision makers when you are *already* in their building!

This is a perfect example of using lemons to make lemonade. It is about seeing the forest through the trees. So, before you fight against scope-creep, **first validate if you can take advantage of it!** I'm known for treating business development like a chess board. Think carefully about these issues before you react to them.

Another example may be a technology solution. Let's assume you are providing all the hardware. Based on the RFP, you and the prime identified the specifications.

But when it is time to order the hardware, the prime tells you that it also needs to have several specifications you were not expecting.

When you tell the prime that you did not price those specifications, they might say:

"Well, those are standard. Sorry if you did not price them but those are the requirements. If you can't get what we need, we will just go with another company."

Similar to the strategy we discussed in the previous chapter, you don't take this lying down. You respond with:

"No, we did not go through weeks of proposal development to lose this work. We both formally discussed the requirements in order to lock-down the scope and specifications. What you are asking for is clearly out of scope."

You need to ask:

"Where did these changes come from? If they came from the government, then here is the cost of those changes and you need to get a change order."

"If these changes are coming from you (the prime), then why did we not know about these during the proposal and pricing phase? Either way, what you are asking for will cost an extra $30,000. That is a major chunk of our margin. At no fault of our own, you are asking us to cover a cost we should not cover."

Bottom line, do not get mad. But do not take it lying down. In this example, the prime knows they made a mistake. The prime does not want to go back to the government and say that they or the government screwed-up. However, if the government changed the specifications after the bid, then the prime needs to go back for a change order.

The prime often makes much more margin and profit than you do. They care about themselves more than you. They care about making money. Do not let them take advantage of you.

There is one situation where you are on your own. If you were solely responsible for scoping out the specifications or requirements and your failure to properly scope causes a major pricing issue, then that is on you.

But if the requirements are being changed and it is outside your control, do not accept it.

I come back to the phrase "It's not about the money. *It's about the money.*"

Think logically. Think like a business professional. Be pragmatic and evaluate the issue without emotion.

If it is not in scope, someone needs to pay for it *or you need to take advantage of it.*

Something to think about.

Chapter 26.
Incumbent Asks You To Prime

T his chapter is packed with strategies and recommendations. During a strategy session, one of our clients received a call from a company that wanted our client to prime a contract. The company that owned the current contract would not be able to bid on the recompete.

To protect both companies, I will use fictitious names. The company that called our client is TechWhite. The opportunity was for a HUBZone set-aside and although TechWhite currently managed the contract, they were not HUBZone.

Let's start there. The incumbent is not HUBZone certified.

My immediate perception? I strongly doubt that TechWhite was doing a good job on the contract.

Why? Because I immediately start wondering why the government would release an acquisition or procurement that makes it impossible for the incumbent to bid on their own contract. If the government liked the job they were doing, they would not have made it impossible for them to bid and prime the recompete.

While it is entirely possible that the agency updated its acquisition strategies, it is possible but not likely. Nine times out of ten, *something is wrong with the incumbent's performance.*

Yes, there can be a good explanation, such as a bundling of contracts or mandated changes in acquisition strategy. But if an incumbent is not allowed to compete on their own contract, it is often safe to say, "Houston, we have a problem."

The next point of interest was that TechWhite was running their contract through several subcontractors. Our client told us that the majority of the full-time employees (FTE) on the contract were from subcontractors. To make matters more interesting, while the incumbent had a couple FTEs on the contract, most of the key positions were subcontracted. My alarm bells were really sounding at this point.

Going off on a tangent, I think this contract fell through the cracks from a federal acquisition regulation (FAR) perspective. I am not convinced that the prime meets the commercially useful function requirements. I really do not believe that TechWhite, the incumbent, should have been awarded this contract in the first place. The original contract was a small-business set-aside and they are doing less than 30% of the work. But I digress.

During discussions with TechWhite, our client said, "Yes, we will prime your contract, giving you 49% of the work, but we need to talk to all the current personnel."

This is completely understandable. You would never prime a contract and use key personnel that you had never spoken to.

TechWhite said, "No. Those are our relationships and if you prime, all the current personnel will still report to us... and we will report to you."

I told our client that was crazy. But they felt it was an opportunity they could not pass up. This situation is not very common, but it happens once or twice a year with our small business clients that are 8a, woman-owned, veteran or HUBZone certified. Companies do not like losing contracts so they do everything in their power to protect half of their contract's revenue.

So even though I recommended they pass on this opportunity, they wanted to move forward and see if they could make it work.

Fair enough.

I told them that since they had a limited time period, they needed to immediately get a teaming agreement (TA) signed. But when they sent the teaming agreement, TechWhite did not want a teaming agreement. They wanted a contract.

TechWhite said, "We want 49% of the contract." Nothing wrong with that. An incumbent can demand that type of percentage. The incumbent has the most detailed and up-to-date intelligence on the opportunity because their people are working those requirements today.

But the incumbent also demanded that the contract include, "if the government does not approve TechWhite as a subcontractor, you will still owe us 49% for the life of the contract."

Our client asked what they should do.

I started laughing.

I told them they needed to think this through. What is unfortunate is that there are many smaller companies that do not recognize the perils, that do not recognize when another company is trying to take them to the cleaners.

Think about TechWhite's demands. It is normal for an incumbent to demand half the contract.

But let's step back for a moment. First, if the government is preventing the incumbent from bidding as prime on their own contract, it is unlikely you will win. The government will find some way of disqualifying your bid or simply picking someone else.

Even though it is the incumbent, do you really want to spend time, money, and energy teaming with them when the government has obviously made it impossible for them to win it on their own? This is the type of intellectual and business though-processes that I want small companies, your company, to think about.

Most companies jump at the chance to prime another company's contract. You may think, "This is an easy win! We have the incumbent on our team!"

What most companies do not consider are the other indirect factors. They do not ask, "Why are they not able to compete on their own contract?" Graduating from the 8a program is an exception.

Let's assume, while highly improbable, that you win the contract with TechWhite. It is possible that you have strong enough past performance that you do not list TechWhite in your proposal. You may have thought, "We're going to team with them for their intelligence but we do not want the government to know they are on the team until after contract award."

I know. That sounds crazy. But companies do it.

But what happens when you have won the contract and the government learns that you are subcontracting to TechWhite? They will find out. They know who currently works for them. Then you get the call, "TechWhite personnel are not authorized to subcontract to you."

Now you need to find another subcontractor to do a chunk of the work. Depending on the key personnel, you may have to forward additional resumes and get government approval.

Now the big question. How are you going to pay the new subcontractor?

Don't forget, you just signed a contract (when you should have signed a teaming agreement) that said you would pay TechWhite forty-nine percent of the revenue *even if the government did not approve them as a subcontractor*!

That statement in the contract now takes on whole new meaning!

How are you going to pay the new subcontractor *and* TechWhite? You can't. You will be hemorrhaging money so fast it will shut down your company.

On a similar but separate requirement, TechWhite also refused to sign exclusivity in the contract. Since exclusivity is fairly standard in federal contracting, this was another red flag. I explained that this was a clear indication that *they are signing multiple and similar contracts with other companies.*

I told TechWhite that priming for an incumbent without asking the right questions is a complete waste of time, money, and manpower. It does not matter how excited you are to get a call from an incumbent. In this case, the incumbent was acting in an unethical and unprofessional manner.

How often does a company try to guarantee revenue even if they are removed from the contract? It does not happen often. I have only seen this happen two or three times during my thirty year career. It is highly unlikely our client would have won this contract anyway. But if they did and TechWhite was booted by the government, the situation could have literally destroyed them.

Now, to have just a bit of fun and create a teachable moment, what if they had won the contract and the government refused to accept TechWhite as a subcontractor? What would I do? I'd tell the government that my company was going to pull out of the contract and explain why. Yes, it would have really angered the government but I'll take the black eye. It was my fault this happened in the first place! So what's the bit of fun in this? Telling TechWhite that we gave the contract back and the government gave the contract to another company. Sure… this situation would have been all my fault. I was less than smart to sign that contract with TechWhite, but if the stars aligned in a manner that would have crushed my company, I would have done the only sensible thing I could to protect myself and my employees.

Thankfully, 24 hours before the proposal was due, we helped our client recognize the dangers and they backed away from the deal.

Regardless, they spent a week on an opportunity that should have been immediately passed-over within hours of being contacted by the incumbent.

We all learn from experience. Our client learned a ton of lessons and we helped educate them on how to approach these type of issues.

The next time you get a call from an incumbent, *do not get stars in your eyes*. Ask the right questions. Ensure it makes sense for your company. Make sure they are not taking advantage of you.

There are many situations where teaming with an incumbent and taking over as prime is a great opportunity. But you have to trust the company you are dealing with and ensure you understand the politics at play.

More than anything, trust your gut!

Something to think about.

Chapter 27.
Debriefings and Audits

Much of what passed in the National Defense Authorization Act (NDAA) will impact calendar years 2018-2020. The impact to small business government procurement is extensive and *positive*.

First, there is a federal agency called the Defense Contract Audit Agency (DCAA). If you have ever won a government contract, odds are you have had to do one of two things. Either you have had to tell the government in your proposal that you are DCAA compliant or right after you won a contract, DCAA sent someone to your office to verify your accounting methods and to perform a pricing audit.

Due to DCAA's role, they are so backlogged that many contractors have been screaming that they are unable to meet solicitation or contract requirements. They cannot get inspected in time.

In response, Congress mandated that the Department of Defense must submit a plan for outsourcing DCAA inspection requirements by October 2018 and then these outsourced services to be up and running by April 2019. The focus would be on closing-out audits for more complex projects.

Why does this matter to you? While the backlog of audits will decrease, there will most likely be *greater scrutiny of your books and pricing*. In other words, getting past an audit will likely be more difficult, especially for smaller businesses.

The next NDAA update impacts post-award debriefings and protests. The Defense Federal Acquisition Regulation (DFARS) will be updated to increase the rights of contractors and what is required as part of a debriefing, which is outstanding for smaller companies! The more you learn in a debriefing the more you can improve and win the next contract.)

If you are new to government contracting, a debriefing is when you have lost a bid and the government explains to you why you lost. Not every solicitation requires a government debrief. Examples of this include GSA Schedule bids or solicitations competed under federal acquisition regulation (FAR) Part 13 for simplified acquisition.

Another update requires that any DoD contract in excess of $100 million requires that the contracting officer provide a redacted copy of the agency's written source selection. This will probably not impact many smaller businesses. But it will for some.

Another update and more applicable to small business is that you now have two days to ask follow-up questions. . . *after* your debriefing. Not only do you have two days after the debrief to send follow-up questions, the agency must respond in writing, not on the phone, within five days. This is already taking place. Several of our clients have forwarded formal debriefings that outlines this process.

In the past you had to be given a debriefing, oral or written, at the discretion of the agency. Then you had 5 days to protest with the agency or GAO if you felt you should have won (or you believe the winning contractor should not have). Contractors do not always receive viable or valuable feedback in their debriefings. So even if you protest, it is a crap-shoot.

Now, not only can you get a debriefing, the government is required to provide redacted written source selection documentation on large procurements. And not only that, you can now follow-up after the debrief, within two days, with additional questions you may have. Then the government *must respond*, in writing, and they have five days to do so.

This process adds potentially seven days from the end of the debrief. Then add another five days at the end of that if there is a desire to protest. That's 12 days. 12 business days and you get more *written* source selection documentation and the ability to ask follow-up questions that must be answered in writing.

These additions will help smaller businesses learn and become more proficient at responding to government solicitations.

The NDAA also requires a change to the DFAR where small business is allowed to obtain source selection documentation for procurements in *excess of $10 million*. It is not clear yet if the DFAR will also allow small business to have 2 days to ask questions after the debrief. We will see as the regulations are updated.

Why is the government making these changes? They are taking these steps in order to *decrease the number of protests*. This is good for the government and it provides more opportunity for small businesses to get additional information on how to be competitive on the next procurement.

Going off on a tangent. If you are not taking advantage of debriefings, start doing so. You get to talk to the government and strengthen your relationship.

You get to find out what you need to improve. You get to find out if there is a perception issue or if one of your past performance write-ups is not as strong as you think it is. **Always ask for a debriefing,** *even if you are not authorized one.* Some contracting officers will provide you with informal feedback.

There is also another update as pertains to protests. The NDAA for 2018 also puts in place a three-year pilot program that requires contractors with $250 million in revenue to reimburse the government for all costs in processing a protest if it is denied in a written opinion. This is not applicable to agency protests. This is primarily GAO and the court of federal claims. Again, this will give some pause to larger companies. Less impact to small business.

As for making larger companies think twice before protesting, we are years away from knowing if this program will work or if it will be passed down to small business. We should see the pilot program going through 2021.

The next update is on low price technically acceptable (LPTA) contracts, which we discussed in Chapter 15. In addition to new regulations, there are two additional circumstances when the Department of Defense (DoD) can now use LPTA.

The first is if DoD believes it will only get minimal or even no additional innovation or technological advantage. The second is if products being procured are expendable in nature.

The latter makes sense. But minimal or no additional innovation? That can be a tricky one. If industry's solutions are de-facto innovative, it is up to the government to decide if LPTA applies. Time will tell if this negatively impacts industry.

So those are a couple of the NDAA's impacts. Some will impact you, such as DCAA, debriefings, and protests. Others may not... at least for a couple years.

Something to think about.

Chapter 28.
Small Business and Proposal Win-Themes

L arger companies have a process, using an online system or Microsoft Excel workbooks with a dozen tabs, that help them understand the government's challenges, their own strengths, and their competition's weaknesses.

Talk to any proposal manager that has worked for a large company and they will tell you the importance of 'win-themes.' They will tell you it is a key reason why they won millions of dollars.

I am often asked by small businesses if win-themes are necessary for small business? Are win themes really necessary for what we sell? We have such a small team.

Now, I both agree and disagree that small businesses should have a formal process for win-themes. How can I both agree and disagree? Let me explain.

Regardless of you selling product or service, win-themes require that you have information and intelligence to be competitive. You have to know if the incumbent is doing a good job. You have to know if your price is competitive. You have to know how your competition is likely to respond to the acquisition. You have to... wait for it... focus your business development activities in pre-acquisition.

So yes. . . many of the activities that companies go through to identify their win-themes are necessary for winning a contract. But in my opinion, smaller companies do not necessarily have to have a formal win-theme process. You need a *formal business development strategy* that collects the same information and intelligence.

The Win Theme Rule

Small businesses don't specifically require a win-them process. But they need a formal business development strategy that captures the same market intelligence.

Larger companies going after large acquisitions must have win-themes. It is how they know they are going down the right path. It is how they know that their proposal and pricing are competitive on $25 million or multi-billion-dollar procurements.

But what about small companies? If you are doing the right sales activities and you are focused on collecting information and intelligence, you are doing the same thing – you are just not calling it a win-theme process.

So yes, whether you are selling copper wire, technology, power tools, or construction services, you need to go through a win-theme process. For smaller businesses, this means you need to have a strong business development strategy.

Win themes are necessary. If you do not have a strong business development process, they are even more important. How formal or informal you make it is based on the maturity of your business development and the value of the opportunity.

For your company, how strong is your business development strategy? How formal do you need your win-theme process to be?

If you want to **consistently** generate revenue, **both** your business development and win-theme strategies need to be strong.

Something to think about.

Chapter 29.
A Major Pricing Mistake in
Your Bid or Proposal

This chapter is about an issue that many companies will experience at one point or another. Imagine that you bid on an opportunity and you win. But when you look at the pricing, you realize that not only did you price it wrong, you have no profit. This happens on occasion when you sell product. Maybe you screwed-up the pricing from the manufacturer when you entered your data in DLA's Internet Bid Board System (DIBBS).

Imagine you bid on a System for Award Management (SAM) opportunity and you win. Your proposal clearly shows you understand all the requirements but with a sense of despair you realize that you forgot to include a key requirement in your pricing.

Just as I was performing the final edits for this book, one of our clients called. They bid $120,000 on a simplified acquisition procurement. They forgot to add $15,000 on one of their service lines. The bid was already turned in. They identified the mistake because the contracting officer called and asked that they clarify a point in their proposal. They had been informally selected to win the contract. Oh boy. $15,000 would eat all of their profit. Now what do you do?

If this has never happened to you, you are lucky. But it will probably happen at some point. If this happens to you, just recognize this is *not* unusual. We are human. We make mistakes.

During the final push of the fiscal year, the government awarded many contracts and over the last several weeks, several of our Federal Access members called asking for help. Each of them made a mistake in their pricing.

What do you do?

There is no right answer but there is a cognitive process you need to go through and then some very specific actions.

First, if you sell product, did you make a mistake in the quantity when you did the pricing. If you did, do you have enough margin to cover your mistake? If you have 13% margin and the cost of covering the difference is less than 13%, you will not take a loss. You may not make much money, but you *will not have to call the contracting officer.*

But if your pricing was for 20 units and your bid is for 35? These mistakes happen much more frequently than you may think. In this case, your pricing does not take into account 15 units. Not only does your margin not cover the mistake, you will actually take a loss on the order. You have no choice. You have to call the contracting officer.

Now, before we talk about companies that provide services, I want to take a step back. Just because the government awards you a contract *does not mean you have to accept the contract.*

Some companies say, "Well, we screwed up and we are not going to get 'black-balled' by the government. We want more orders from this agency so we will accept the loss and chalk it up to experience." This is what is called a loss-leader. I *never* recommend a company accept loss-leaders.

You made a mistake. You are human. Many contracting officers will be frustrated but they will also understand the situation. So please do not take a loss on your bids. If you make a mistake, own it and fix it.

Will some contracting officers "remember you" and purposely not give you an award next time? Sure. It happens. Business is business and most contracting officers are understanding - not vindictive. You may lose the order. They may put it back out for bid. They may simply award it to the next company.

The same applies to service companies. Imagine you are a security company that provides hardware and installation for access control, intrusion detection, and video surveillance. You submit a bid. You understand the requirements. You flew across the country and attended industry day.

However, you or your team made a mistake and forgot to include the hardware and installation costs for one of the 15 hallways in the building. It is a $900,000 contract and the one hallway costs $150,000.

The odds are you won the contract due to pricing. It is unlikely the other contractors made a similar mistake.

There is no way your margins can cover this. But unlike bids that are only for product sales, you will ask the following question. "If you end-up breaking-even or maybe your profit is just a couple thousand dollars, is it worth it?" Can you afford to have an installation team of five employees working on a project for three weeks and the company makes minimal to no profit?

So even if your margins can support a pricing mistake on a services contract, can your company afford to work, at no profit, for three weeks? The answer is probably no.

What do you do?

First, hopefully you caught the pricing mistake before you ship the product or before you initiate services.

Your first priority is to talk to the contracting officer in person. If they are local, go see them. If they are across the country, whether or not you get on a plane will depend on the value of the contract.

If it is a $12,000 contract, you are probably not flying across the country. But if it is a million-dollar contract, you get on a plane. $1,000 for airfare and lodging is worth every penny to protect a contract with $80,000 in profit.

By the way, whether local or not, do not tell the contracting officer why you need to see them. Simply say you need to talk to them in person. If they press you, say it is about the recently awarded contract and there is an issue you want to discuss face to face.

If you have to have that conversation by phone, then do it. But contracting officers are *much more likely to accept your mistake* if you make the time to see them face to face.

When you talk to them, *fall on your sword*. Tell them you screwed-up. Mea culpa. Mea culpa. Mea culpa. Tell them you need help. You made an honest mistake.

For the product company, you can offer to provide the 15 units at manufacturer cost. You will take no profit on those units. That is absolutely fair and shows the government that you will own the mistake.

For the service company, you can offer all the equipment for the missed hallway at no profit, the same as the product example above. But you do not have the same flexibility for your employees. You have to charge for labor. But again, for that one hallway, tell the government you'll cut your margin by 50%. Again, that is fair. This may give you enough wiggle room for the contracting officer to make a contract mod. It's also very possible that the solicitation will be put for bid again.

You simply need to open-up a dialogue, fall on your sword, and make it crystal clear that you feel horrible but want to make it right.

If the contracting officer is unwilling to work with you, be prepared to lose the contract. It is not their fault that you are in this situation. Also, do not assume they will recompete the contract. They may simply select the next contractor based on source selection.

In the long term, losing the contract is better than accepting a contract and losing money.

Government employees, including contracting officers are just like you. They tie their shoes the same way you do. Initially, you will freak-out. Just calm down and think about the issue in a logical manner.

More often than not, you will keep the contract. You just won't make as much money.

Something to think about.

Chapter 30.
Red Fish. Blue Fish.
Bid-Matching and Other Tools

D o you use a bid-matching tool to identify government opportunities? How about a customer relationship management (CRM) tool to manage your pipeline, prospects, and clients? How many Microsoft Excel spreadsheets do you use? Perhaps one for teaming; one for prospects; one for pipeline? Does your company have an online network-drive where everyone updates these various documents?

In this chapter, I want to talk about the free and paid tools and resources you obtain from various companies that support government contractors.

Does this sound familiar?

"We use three different bid-matching tools to find opportunities. One is free, we pay for two, but one is industry specific for what we sell. We use our bid-matching tools and the Federal Procurement Data System (FPDS) / SAM and USASpending.gov for contract and data research. We use a CRM (e.g. Zoho or Salesforce) to track our leads, our opportunities, and to manage our pipeline. We have two Microsoft Excel workbooks that we use for managing other requirements. We also have three consultants working with us, one full time and two hourly when we need them."

I did not mention Microsoft Outlook or whichever email system you use. If you think about the tools your company uses on a daily basis, you probably have several more.

There are many companies, especially smaller companies, that want to try everything. I call it the **gold fish syndrome**. "Oh look! That will help me win contracts! Oh, look at that! We need to use it. This tool and this tool and that tool will help us win a contract!"

There is nothing wrong with wanting to improve your processes and operations. There is nothing wrong with trying new tools. My company, RSM Federal, provides many tools that accelerates the lessons in this book. But *your strategy* should drive *which tools and resources you need*. Do not let your tools drive your strategy or your daily activities!

It is very easy to get lost in your tools because it is easier than calling prospects. For most business developers, selling is not a skill they are born with. You might have awesome communication skills, but learning to sell takes practice, patience, and experience.

Since many professionals in a sales role are uncomfortable selling, what do you think most of them fall back on? They fall back on entering data into spreadsheets and searching their bid-matching tools. Why? Because it's easy. You have instant gratification. *But tracking your data does not win contracts.*

If all you are doing is reviewing opportunities on SAM and then entering data into your pipeline or CRM, all you are performing is "death by administration."

Don't Create Chaos

Then there are companies that blast 'ideas' to everyone on their team. Every marketing and business development strategy they find gets forwarded to their management or sales team.

As soon as you register in the System for Award Management (SAM) you get hammered with marketing emails from companies that guarantee millions of dollars in government contracts. Every time you attend an event or conference, you receive free advice and strategies. Hey, I do this as well! You want to ensure that you learn who provides real value and who does not. When you Google 'government sales' there are thousands of free and paid resources.

I have seen quite a few business owners that forward every 'great idea' or sales strategy to their team. "Hey, this could be the reason why we aren't winning as many contracts."

Every week they find a new concept and forward these articles or strategies to their managers or business developers.

Stop doing this!

This confuses your management and sales team. Every time you forward a new whitepaper on how to sell to the government; how to win a contract in Q4; or how to position for sole source awards, you are *creating chaos for your team.*

Yes! Education is the difference between a job and an occupation. If you have ever attended one of my seminars, you know that I believe education and life-long-learning are critical to success.

But every time you forward "great ideas" to your sales team it looks like you are recommending a new strategy or new sales tactic. *This is a recipe for disaster.* You have to step back and question whether you are improving your overall strategy or making it more confusing.

Here is what you do not want – "*Here is our strategy, but this looks really promising! Let's try this!*" or "*I just downloaded this seven-step guide. It was free, from an email I just received. . . and it has nothing to do with our current strategy... but maybe this will help us.*"

Have you heard the phrase, "hope is not a strategy?" (I've only used it half a dozen times already in this book.) Well, the same goes for "maybe is not a strategy." Do not tell your team that something might help them achieve their goals.

Find the one or two resources that you trust implicitly. Build your market and sales strategy *and then execute it.* Do not stop every couple days or weeks to question your strategy or forward a bunch of ideas to your sales team. Do not forward anything unless you have qualified how those resources or strategies will impact the guidance you have already given your team. If you don't do this, you are going to confuse them!

There is a difference between continuously educating your team and bogging them down with conflicting information and guidance from multiple sources.

Recommendation: most companies have an offsite once or twice a year. Collect those great ideas and resources, evaluate which ones you want your team to see, and then use the offsite to present several of those concepts.

Don't Operate in a Vacuum

Let's start this section with a general statement. Not every company needs a coach or consultant. Many companies do well with their counselor at the Procurement Technical Assistance Center (PTAC).

Whether free or paid, the average company only needs one coach or consultant to help them position for and win contracts. On occasion you will have two but the second consultant either has a relationship you want to take advantage of or is in an advantageous geographic location. For the average small business, if you need a business coach or consultant for government sales, one strong consultant is all you need.

Allow me to go off on another tangent. Every company has at one point in time or another hired a consultant. If you had a bad experience, it is because you did not do your due diligence. To be fair, you don't know what you don't know and sometimes it's a painful lesson.

There are as many bad consultants as there are good ones. 95% of our clients win contracts. That is not a bold unsubstantiated allegation. I can prove it. But most coaches and consultants do not have that kind of track record. So, if a day comes when you are ready to hire someone to help you accelerate your sales, whoever you hire, make sure you get four (4) referrals and call every single one of them! Make sure they have a solid track-record.

If you use multiple consultants, *do not let them operate in a vacuum*! Imagine for a moment, two consultants working for your company. When both are giving the same advice, it is awesome. Do you really need duplicate feedback and guidance? If you have more than one coach or consultant, I guarantee you are getting conflicting guidance. Now your team doesn't know who to trust or which recommendations they should apply.

So, if you use more than one consultant, those two consultants *should be introduced to each other* and you need to ensure they have fields of responsibility. Each one should be responsible for **different outcomes**. Otherwise, you are wasting money and creating chaos for your team.

Obvious exception to the one-coach-rule would be if you have engaged the Procurement Technical Assistance Center (PTAC) which provides free guidance and support to small business government contractors. In this example, probably 40% of my clients also work with their local PTAC. In some situations, we are all working together! More than half a dozen state PTACs work with the same companies I work with. *We work together.*

It is always better if everyone supporting a company knows each other. Better communication. Stronger guidance. Faster acceleration into the market.

To learn more about small business coaches and consultants, I have included a chapter with recommendations and where I outline various challenges.

Bid-Matching Tools

Another one of the tools that you use in government sales is a bid-matching tool. They are also called contract management systems. These are the tools that send you daily or weekly emails of opportunities that you can bid on.

If you are going to pay for a bid-matching tool, you only need to pay for one. Pick the right one and use it correctly. If you are new to the market or you have been in the market for several years, start with the bid-matching tool provided by your local Procurement Technical Assistance Center (PTAC).

As always, there are exceptions to every rule. An example would be an industry specific bid-matching tool. Two of our clients, a plumbing supply company and a hardware and electronics superstore, both pay for industry specific bid-matching tools. Both companies increased their *visibility* on opportunities by 30% and increased revenue by 20%.

Yes, there are other advanced bid-matching tools but do not spend money on them unless you already have a strong business development process. The PTAC's bid-matching tool is free. I will go into much more detail on the costs of these tools and how to properly use them in the next chapter.

When it comes to market research, no bid-matching tool replaces the Federal Procurement Data System (FPDS) / SAM [23] or USASpending.gov –

---

[23] FPDS is migrating into the Integrated Award Environment (IAE) and will be

203

both of which are free. Bid-matching tools, when used properly, provide outstanding value. There are currently more than 500 available on the market today. They all pull data from the same free government systems. The difference is that they crunch data in different ways. Much of what you pay for in the expensive bid-matching systems is the back-end and user-interface, how these companies aggregate and display the data in ways that help companies position for contracts. This is why you have to test specifically for what you sell.

There will often be times when you are looking for something very specific and a bid-matching tool might not help you. Remember, these systems all pull data from the same data sources. This is why no matter what bid-matching tool you use; you *always* want to know how to use FPDS / SAM for researching historical government contract data. USASpending.gov is a great system but USASpending.gov pulls its data *from FPDS / SAM* among other systems. Also, USASpending.gov does not pull all the data from FPDS / SAM.

You need to learn how to use FPDS / SAM! I've already mentioned this several times but if you need training videos, basic and advanced, with step-by-step strategies on how to use FPDS / SAM, visit the Federal Access (FA) Knowledge-Base and Training Platform (www.rsmfederal.com/FA). You will also learn how to manipulate the contract data using Microsoft Excel pivot tables.

Time for me to go off on yet another tangent. There are companies that sell bid-matching tools where the bid-matching tool also provides Customer Relationship Management (CRM) (sales pipeline) functionality. In my opinion, there might only be half-a-dozen (out of 500) bid-matching tools that I would recommend for CRM functionality. Furthermore, only a few have mapped their functionality to how a company **should operate from a business perspective**.

Let's say that again. Only a few have mapped their functionality to how a company **should operate from a business perspective**.

---

part of System for Award Management (SAM) in 2020.

If these bid-matching tools had best-in-class CRM capability, they would not be bid-matching tools. They would be CRM tools. Nothing wrong with trying to build the next mouse-trap. Everyone is trying to make money.

Another one of my frustrations are small businesses paying for a bid-matching system that *focuses on their workflow* and not contract and opportunity data.

I don't blame bid-matching companies that try to focus on your workflow and sales cycle. They do this to differentiate from other bid-matching companies. But that is not their primary competency. *That is not what they are good at.* That is not the value you are looking for from a bid-matching tool.

Let me give you an example. There is a bid-matching company that has tried to automate your sales cycle. They have developed a bid-matching system that with the click of a button, will create and email your response to a sources-sought. Think about that. That is amazing.

But if it really worked, they would be the next Amazon.

Here's the thing. It does work. It sends a document to the government with your company information. Go back to what we discussed in Chapter 4 on Ghosting Requirements to Influence the Acquisition. You know that the only way to successfully respond to a sources-sought is to **tailor and ghost requirements**. Your objective is to *influence the acquisition*. If all you do is answer the government's questions and give your corporate information, *you are not influencing the acquisition!*

This is an excellent example of really cool technology that *completely fails* to support smart business strategy. If you currently use a bid-matching tool that provides workflow for your business development activities and you like it, great! But ask yourself, "While I have these capabilities, do they really help me position for and *influence the acquisition*?"

My point is this - you pay for a bid matching tool because of the data it provides and how it presents that data to you. I understand why bid-matching companies create additional functionality. Some of this additional functionality is awesome!

But for some capabilities, while it works from a technological perspective, it often does not work from a business perspective.

> *It is not a question of 'if' the tool works. It is a question of 'whether or not it provides the value you need.'*

Do not get side-tracked by the extra bells and whistles. If you are getting a bid-matching tool, get it for its bid-matching. I would ignore the other functionality. That is not what they are good at. That is not what you need.

If you are wondering which bid-matching tools I think are the best, I am going to leave you hanging. It depends on what you sell. If you do not have one, always start with the PTAC's free bid-matching tool. Remember, they all pull data from the same systems.

As for CRMs, you can get an awesome online CRM and pipeline tool for $25 a month.

Getting Handcuffed to a System

Also, most bid-matching companies want you to spend as much time in their system as possible. They want you to use their system for everything. The more time you spend in their system, the more likely you will be forced to renew your license next year.

Think about this for a minute! You paid for a bid-matching tool but you will be held hostage in a year when you realize all your important prospecting data is in that system! It is a brilliant client-retention strategy. I cannot fault these companies for this practice.

I recommend you keep your pipeline, contact information, and notes in a CRM, separate from your bid-matching tool.

Summary

Let's summarize. No more than one consultant unless you have them working together. No more than one paid bid-matching tool unless one is industry focused. Have one CRM for pipeline and managing your contacts, notes, and opportunities.

If you want to keep confusing your team, just keep forwarding all that "great information." Unless you have evaluated the impact against the guidance you have already given your team, all you are doing is creating chaos.

If you use all of these tools and resources, but you do not make phone calls to the government and talk to people, all of these resources are a *waste of time and money.*

All the tools in the world do not replace making calls, and building relationships. This goes for your government prospects as well as your teaming partners.

Have you developed a strategy and you are executing it?

The tools and resources you use are **simply tools**.

Your sale's strategy drives which tools and resources your team will use.

Something to think about.

Chapter 31.
The Truth About Bid-Matching Tools

I am a voracious reader. My wife and I converted the dining room in our house into a library. We have more than 5,000 books on wall-to-wall bookshelves.

When I buy a business book, I immediately look at the table of contents and look for chapters I want to read. This is even easier when it is an eBook. First published in January 2019, this book was released both paperback and on Amazon Kindle. [24]

Whether you purchased the paperback or eBook, you probably reviewed the table of contents. I will also hazard-to-guess that 70% of readers jumped straight to this chapter. Why? Because the truth about bid-matching tools is one of the most listened-to podcast episodes on Game Changers for Government Contractors.

Oh, here's some exciting news! If you like this book; if you like hearing about tactics and strategies from subject matter experts, two items. First, if you're not already a listener of the podcast Game Changers for Government Contractors, head over to rsmfederal.com, iTunes, or Sound Cloud. Second, shortly after the release of this book, the book Game Changers will be released on Amazon. It consists of almost thirty (30) subject matter experts, all of whom have been guests on the Game Changer's podcast.

If you're a hound for information and you're constantly looking to educate yourself on getting stronger in government sales, consider the following resources:

---

[24] This second edition will also be available via audio book (Amazon Audible) in early 2020.

- Book - An Insider's Guide to Winning Government Contracts (this book).
- Podcast - Game Changers for Government Contractors (iTunes and Soundcloud).
- Book - Game Changers for Government Contracts (releases February 2020)
- Federal Access Knowledge-Base and Training Platform (rsmfederal.com)
- Manual - The Government Sales Manual on Amazon

So, if you jumped straight to this chapter, I recommend you read the previous chapter before you continue. The previous chapter is *Red Fish. Blue Fish. Bid-Matching and Other Tools*.

Of the thirty odd seminars and training courses I give on government sales, how to use bid-matching tools is a common discussion topic. In my role as an adjunct faculty instructor for Govology, I presented a seminar called Winning Strategies for Government Prospecting. In this seminar I discuss twenty prospecting methods that fall into three categories of Weak, Strong, and Core.

Bid-matching tools fall within the weak category, not because they are not useful, but because companies often fail to properly use them.

Bid-matching tools are also called bid-matching systems or contract management systems. They help you identify opportunities to bid on.

If you have been in the market for even six months, you will know that your local procurement technical assistance center (PTAC) will give you access to their bid-matching system for free. Free makes the PTAC tool the least expensive of the bid-matching tools on the market.

Almost all bid-matching tools are a subscription model where you pay monthly or annually for access. At a premium level, there are three or four that are household names. I will list several of the premium tools, not because I endorse them, like them, or dislike them. They all provide some level of value. But I want to make sure that you understand what I mean when I say a bid-matching system. I am talking about systems such as Deltek's GovWin, and Bloomberg. Deltek's GovWin is the 800-pound gorilla.

However, a lot of companies cannot afford to spend $6,000 to $18,000 on a bid-matching tool. Most companies do not use the premium tools. They use the basic and mid-tier solutions.

For this discussion, it does not matter whether you are looking at a basic or premium tool. It does not matter if you're using the PTAC's bid-matching tool or Deltek's GovWin. Before you use or pay for one of these tools, you need to understand how these tools support your business development and sales process.

---

*These tools, by themselves, **do not win contracts**.*

To repeat what I outlined in the previous chapter, you should always start-out in government sales using the PTAC's bid-matching tool. It provides all the basic information you need to start your journey. There are thousands of companies that grow their federal business and continue to use the PTAC's tool. Bottom line, the expensive and more feature-rich systems should not be used unless your company has a strong business development process.

I cannot over-emphasize this enough. Unless you are performing the *right business development activities*, these systems will be nothing more than a waste of time and money.

There are always a half-a-dozen folks who attend my sessions that work for bid-matching companies. They often approach me afterwards, frustrated with me, because I make it a little more difficult for them to sell licenses for their tools. Let's not kid anyone. I am only one person. Yes, I am one of many national voices for small companies that sell to the government, but I highly doubt my opinion is wide-spread enough to impact the sales for these companies.

My intent is not to impact their sales. My intent is to educate companies on what it takes to successfully win government contracts.

Even though these bid-matching companies may be frustrated with my sessions, most agree with my position on this. If you do not have a strong business development process, no tool or amount of data is going to make a difference.

If you do not understand how to engage opportunities in pre-acquisition; if you don't have a formal plan for calling the government and collecting intelligence; if you do not attend government events, industry days and conferences; and if you do not move opportunities through your pipeline so that you are more competitive... then it does not matter if you use a free bid-matching system or a $6,000 one. You are not going to win many contracts. One of the reasons I wrote this book was to help you ask the right questions!

Many bid-matching companies want you to believe that by using their tool you will have a competitive advantage; that you will win more contracts. What they do not tell you is that unless you have a very strong business development strategy, the tools provide *less value*. They are not going to tell you this. They want you to pay for their tool. But from a business perspective, you need to understand the dynamics between these tools and a strong sales strategy.

The premium tools will allow you to see what the contracting officers have said about the opportunity. You can see copies of various documents that provide background on the opportunity.

But remember this - everyone using that tool has access to the *exact same information*. Is it giving you a competitive advantage? Sure, against companies that do not use that tool. But at least a dozen to several hundred other companies going after that request for proposal (RFP) use the same tool. They have the same information.

Unless you are collecting information and intelligence outside this tool during pre-acquisition, *your competitive advantage is neutralized*.

Don't get me wrong. I have used more than a dozen bid-matching tools, including every premium tool, during my career. My company currently uses one of the premium tools. It absolutely provides value. But you should not be paying big bucks for a bid-matching tool unless you have a strong market strategy.

These tools will not fix your lack of sales. They may give you a small competitive edge, but not one strong enough to communicate competitive advantage in your bid or proposal.

So, if you do not have a strong sales process, stick with the free or less expensive tools.

If you have a strong sales process, odds are you are winning contracts and can afford the premium tools.

Make sure you have realistic expectations.

These tools are just... tools.

Something to think about.

Chapter 32.
Productivity Tools
Stop Relying on Them!

T his chapter reinforces several of the earlier chapters. I may be beating a dead horse, but I don't believe this can be overemphasized.

Let's start-off where the last chapter ended - bid-matching tools. Companies both experienced and new to the market often spend *way too much time* sorting through 'opportunity emails' instead of focusing on pre-acquisition strategies. In other words, stop spending hours every day reviewing opportunities to bid on. Instead, focus on building relationships with your prospects.

Companies that spend most of their time searching for opportunities struggle to win contracts. Companies that spend most of their time building relationships and influencing acquisitions are multi-million-dollar companies.

Then you have customer relationship management (CRM) and pipeline tools. It is not uncommon for the less experienced to spend a couple hours every day updating and capturing their notes. Nothing wrong with updating your opportunities and pipeline, but it should *not* be a full-time job. It should *not* be a part-time job.

Between updating pipelines, CRMs, searching your bid-matching tool, and sorting through opportunity emails, you want to make sure you are not spending all your time in data capture.

Many small business professionals, especially business developers, don't know what they don't know. This is normal. Until they have been taught how to properly perform business development, they often hide behind their computer. Again, this is normal. If you are the owner of a company, you have to make sure your business developers are maturing and performing the right sale's activities.

Why do so many business developers spend so much time on these activities? Because it is their comfort zone. Calling prospects and collecting intelligence is perceived to be more time consuming and frustrating. Many business developers get stuck in their comfort zone.

"Hey boss! Look at all the work I have been doing. You can see all the updates I've made on the pipeline, in the CRM. I have reviewed more than 100 opportunities this week!"

You are not going to win your next contract if all you are doing is using these tools and staying in your comfort zone.

As mentioned previously, in addition to running RSM Federal, I am also an adjunct faculty instructor for Govology. I provide webinars, every month, for companies that work with their local PTAC. If you need help with getting out of the "comfort zone," attend my webinars and use the strategies and templates in Federal Access (FA).

One of the webinars in Federal Access is called 'Winning Strategies for Government Prospecting.' I provide step-by-step strategies for the three core prospecting activities that are much more important than these online tools.

What are the three core activities? First, you have to focus on pre-acquisition activities, not waiting for the RFPs and RFQs to be released. Second, you need to have a strong programmatic teaming strategy. And third, you have to connect with and talk to contracting officers and government decision makers.

Simple - yet complicated.

If you do not perform these three activities, you are not going to collect competitive intelligence. It will be difficult to achieve a competitive position. You will have difficulty ghosting your strengths and the weakness of your competition. You will not be influencing the acquisition.

All of these tools you use? They will help capture information and intelligence and help you track what you are doing. But they will not provide you with a competitive advantage.

I want you to think about the activities you are doing every day and how much time you are spending on each one.

If only 10% of your time is focused on pre-acquisition; influencing procurements through sources-sought; talking to other companies; and talking to government influencers and decision makers, then these tools are nothing more than a waste of time and money.

They say the truth hurts. Perhaps it does.

Are you stuck in a 'comfort zone?'

Are you focused on building relationships in pre-acquisition?

What will it take to refocus your efforts?

Something to think about.

Chapter 33.
Strong Relationships
Drive Strong Opportunities

This lesson provides insight on how seasoned sales professionals approach the federal market. We are going to discuss where successful companies find qualified opportunities. We are going to run through several of the most common online government systems that government contractors use to find opportunities to bid on.

Whether you are new to the market or been in the market for years, it is sometimes nice to have affirmation that you are doing the right things.

While most of what I am going to cover may sound familiar, I am going to make two important points at the end of the chapter that you may not have considered. This requires that I set-up the discussion so I am going to start with reviewing the various systems where you can find opportunities.

Most companies that start off in government sales are told to go to the System for Award Management (https://sam.gov/SAM/). Any product or service that is more than $25,000 in sales is normally found in SAM.

If you sell product, many companies automatically think GSA Schedule and the online buyer's portal at GSA Advantage. However, it is rare for the majority of any product to be sold on a GSA Schedule. Yes exceptions exist but you'll need to validate it yourself base on what you sell.

A GSA Schedule is just an acquisition vehicle. It is one of many acquisition vehicles. By the way, if you have a GSA Schedule, make sure all your products are properly loaded into GSA Advantage and if you provide services, make sure your labor categories (and products) are loaded into the GSA eLibrary. If you don't have a GSA Schedule, let's not forget that you can look up the competitive price points for your competition's products and / or services in these systems!

If you want to respond to GSA Schedule procurements, you have to have a schedule (yes, that is obvious), but having a schedule also gives you access to GSA eBuy. For those new to GSA Schedules and the systems that support them, don't worry. It can seem a bit overwhelming at first but it's fairly simple.

GSA eBuy is another contract management system. Everyone has access to SAM. But only GSA Schedule holders have access to GSA eBuy to see real-time GSA Schedule bid opportunities.

If you haven't seen GSA Advantage, make a note to visit it, poke around, and see what other companies are selling and how much they charge. For product companies, this is a great place to find competitive intelligence and pricing.

If you sell medical supplies, you may want to consider getting a VA Schedule. It is similar to a GSA Schedule but managed by Veterans Affairs.

Now, if you primarily sell products, you really need to investigate DLA's Internet Bid Board System (DIBBS). It is free to access. You'll need a SAM account before registering. The procurements on DIBBS (primarily products and commodities), are in the billions of dollars every year.

Okay, so far, we have covered SAM, Federal Supply Schedules (FSS), both GSA and VA, and DIBBS.

But there is also an online shopping mall called FedMall. This used to be called DoD eMall (back in the day when dinosaurs were about). Like DIBBS, it is managed by the Defense Logistics Agency (DLA).

You also want to remember that the government uses blanket purchase agreements (BPA) as well as other multiple award contracts (MAC) and multiple award task order contracts (MATOC).

Blanket purchase agreements can be given to just one company but are often given to two or more companies. Some blanket purchase agreements are only awarded to companies that have GSA Schedules. Other blanket purchase agreements are open market (requires no specific contract vehicle). There is no set standard. It depends on how the agency or contracting officer wants to award it.

There are so many ways for the government to purchase what you sell. But the last paragraph made an important point. It depends on how the agency or contracting officer wants to award it.

Influence the Acquisition
Strong relationships build strong opportunities.

And finally, you have category management.

Both federal agencies and the armed services are using this extensively. Category management is tied to strategic sourcing where the government wants to decrease the number of government contractors that are authorized to bid on a requirement and in doing so, the government negotiates the best pricing it can from those select companies for an extended period of time.

If you want to learn more about strategic sourcing and category management, I published an article on LinkedIn called *The Future of Government Contracting* (you'll find it on my LinkedIn profile). If you are the type that prefers to hear something versus reading it, the article was also published as a podcast. Visit the Podcast Game Changers for Government Contractors on iTunes or Soundcloud.

Furthermore, due to the speed in which category management is taking over government acquisition, this edition of the book includes a new chapter on category management! If you skipped Chapter 9, I strongly recommend that you go back and take a look. Next to the chapter on Ghosting, the chapter on Category Management is incredibly important. It's the future of the entire government's acquisition strategy.

So, you have SAM which everyone can access. You have federal supply schedules that includes government access via GSA Advantage (for products) and having access to the GSA eBuy bidding system (for products and services).

Anyone can use DIBBS (for products) which is managed by the Defense Logistics Agency.

You have the online shopping center for the Department of Defense called FedMall (for products).

You have blanket purchase agreements, MACs, MATOCS, and category management acquisition initiatives which may or may not require that you have a GSA Schedule.

Yes, there are other systems and acquisition vehicles and at first, it is difficult to figure out which systems give you the best bang for the buck. You have to research each system, poke around, and see which systems or acquisition vehicles are *used the most for what you sell*.

If you need help figuring out which systems you should use, start with your local PTAC. If you want additional strategies on how to bid on these opportunities and systems, you can look at the Federal Access Knowledge-Base.

By the way, notice that I have not mentioned reverse auctions. I strongly recommend against using them unless you are seeing hundreds of thousands or millions of dollars in acquisitions for what you sell. Even then, be very wary! Of all the systems we have discussed, reverse auction sites *will* give you the lowest margins. They are primarily in the best interests of the government, *not the contractor*.

In Chapter 15 we discussed low price technically acceptable (LPTA) contracts. Reverse auctions are the epitome of LPTA. I recommend that most companies stay away from them.

Now, two final points. All of these systems are just that - *systems*. As I have said repeatedly in earlier chapters, none of them replace the business development and relationship activities you must perform to be successful in the government market.

Yes, I've made this point a dozen different ways in the previous chapters.

Yes, companies make millions and billions of dollars using them but many of their sales come from agencies that know who they are.

Second, why are relationships so important? Why is it so important that government buyers know who you are? One reason is micro-purchases. This is more applicable if your company sells products but there are tens of thousands of small companies that provide services for smaller projects.

I touch-on micro-purchases in several chapters. A micro-purchase is when a government buyer uses their credit card to buy your products or services. The micro-purchase threshold is currently $10,000 for both federal agencies and the Department of Defense (DoD). Just several years ago the thresholds were in the $2,500 to $3,000 range. The increase to these thresholds also means that government buyers are *more incentivized* to use their credit cards. NOTE [25]

Micro-purchases are not publicly listed. The government knows who sells what they need. This means that *you* should be focused on letting buyers know who you are.

In addition to micro-purchase, there are also simplified acquisition procedures (SAP) that fall under FAR Part 13. If you're new to government sales, don't worry about remembering Federal Acquisition Regulation (FAR) Part 13. Just remember that SAP procurements are specifically set-aside for small business and you can sell a good amount of product or services at the SAP threshold of $250,000. I discussed how to find procurements and agencies that use SAP procedures in Chapter 11.

Simply having a GSA or VA Schedule, having an account on DIBBS or FedMall, using SAM, or any of these other systems is not going to help you consistently win micro-purchase orders.

The most important point of this chapter is that the relationships you build with buyers is one-hundred times more important than having a GSA Schedule or using government systems to find and bid on opportunities.

Figure out which systems are best for what you sell. If you focus on all of them, you will waste two to three hours every day looking for opportunities. Spending all your time behind a computer is not going to get you any closer to consistently winning government contracts.

Regardless of the systems you use, you need to ask yourself:

How strong is my business development strategy?

Am I building the right relationships with government buyers?

---

[25] Credit Cards are issued to all government buyers under the GSA SmartPay program. SmartPay is a program where the contractors are the issuing banks (Bank of America, US Bank, Citigroup, etc.) that have signed agreements with MasterCard or Visa to specifically support the government market.

So, where do you find strong opportunities? Not in bid-matching tools or online government systems. Your strongest opportunities are the ones where you have built a strong relationship with the agency and spent several months focused on pre-acquisition activities in order to influence the acquisition.

Something to think about.

Chapter 34.
Small Business Offices

F or the Department of Defense, the Office of Small Business Programs (OSBP) is charged with helping you learn how to sell to the Department of Defense. Most military installations and major commands have an office. For federal agencies, the Office of Small Disadvantaged Business Utilization (OSDBU) performs the same functions. Bottom line, if you are new to government sales, small business offices are an important touch-point.

I have said this time and again, every individual and organization you touch are a microcosm of society. You have the good and the bad. To be clear, federal agency small business offices provide a critical function and service.

You may walk into one agency's small business office and walk out with a ton of valuable information. You walk into another agency's small business office and you walk-out wondering why you wasted your time. This is normal. It is like anything else in the world. Some are better than others. Do not blow-off the small business offices simply because you had a bad experience with one.

There is one very specific question you need to answer for each small business office. The answer to this question will tell you how much influence that counselor or specialist has with their agency. The question is:

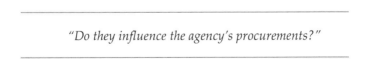

"Do they influence the agency's procurements?"

You do not want to ask this question directly. Ask questions about their relationships with the contracting offices. Ask them whether or not they get to see sources-sought, RFPs, and RFQs *before they are released on SAM.*

To better understand this, let's use an example. Several years ago, the Director of the Small Business Program Office for U.S. Transportation Command (USTRANSCOM), was a woman by the name of Michelle Mendez. A phenomenal talent and champion for small business.

Michelle took over the small business office for one of our country's eleven joint commands. If you're familiar with joint commands, you may be thinking, "Wait... I thought there were ten joint commands?" Well, I would have thought the same thing until only a few weeks ago. The President signed the order to stand-up the United States Space Command (USSPACECOM).

Every U.S. military unit falls within one or more of these eleven commands. So being the small business director for a combatant / joint command means that she represents major commands that includes components from the Army, Navy, Air Force, and Marines. If you ever hear someone say, "It's a purple command," purple refers to more than one military service. Purple is synonymous with the word "Joint." It is a joint command. It is a purple command.

Michelle already had strong relationships with the various contracting offices within the command. She developed a process and strategy where many of the contracting officers would send her drafts of solicitations before they were released on FedBizOpps (now SAM) NOTE [26] and other sources. If she felt that an acquisition should be set-aside for small business, 8(a), WOSB, or SDVOSB, *she would recommend that the contracting officer modify their acquisition strategy.*

That is influence! She influenced hundreds if not thousands of acquisitions. This is the type of small business specialist you want to find at government agencies and with the military commands.

If you meet with a small business specialist and all they do is tell you to send them your capability statement, that specialist is not likely to influence

---

[26] For decades, FedBizOpps (FBO) was the central location for all government opportunities in excess of $25,000. In November 2019, GSA migrated all FBO functionality into the System for Award Management (SAM). FBO, as well as FPDS, and other systems are all being integrated into the Integrated Award Environment (IAE).

the agency's procurements. If all they say is to visit the agency website and then direct you to SAM, you are not going to be influencing procurements.

You want to find those that can influence the acquisition cycle. It will be hit or miss. Some will provide more value than others.

What if they do not have relationships with the contracting officers? Does that mean they they there is no value to be found? Of course not. They will help you understand the basics of selling to and supporting their agency or command. They might even introduce you to the buyers! If a small business specialist at Homeland Security facilitated a meeting with the program manager that buys what you sell, do you really care if the small business office has influence with their contracting officers?

They may not know the contracting officers, but they may know your buyers. That is another important type of influence!

If you find a small business director or specialist that knows your buyers and works in tandem with the contracting officers to reviews solicitations before they get released, *that is a gold mine*. Grow and protect that relationship.

Ask the right questions.

If you find a good resource, hang on tight and take advantage of them.

We are *all* a microcosm of society.

Something to think about.

Chapter 35.
Business Coaches and Consultants

L ions and tigers and bears. There are good and bad lawyers; good and bad teachers; good and bad police officers. For every profession, some are good at what they do and others… are not so good.

Every company, at one time or another, has hired a consultant they wish they had never heard of. Almost every company experiences the 'bad consultant.'

There are only three sure things in life.

Taxes, Death, and a Bad Consultant.

There are two things you should consider after meeting with a consultant or business coach. First, do they understand business?

You Need Both Sides of the Value Chain
Just because someone is an expert in government acquisition does not make them an expert in business, in sales, in marketing, in corporate operations, or in business strategy.

Take a step back. Just because someone is an expert in government acquisition does *not* make them an expert in business, in sales, in marketing, in corporate operations, or in business strategy.

There are thousands of consultants, mentors, small business offices, specialists, and counselors in a wide range of for-profit and non-profit organizations. They might be former military officers, former contracting officers, or former government buyers. A number of former government employees become business consultants. It makes sense! They know companies are looking for help navigating the government's acquisition process.

However, just because someone understands government acquisition does not mean they understand how a company needs to position and sell. It only means that *they might understand one side of the value chain – being the buyer.*

The same goes for consultants. Just because someone worked for a company that sold to the government does not mean they understand the government market. It only means *they might understand one side of the value chain – being the seller.*

No matter who you work with, you need *both* sides of the value chain. They will understand not only what you need to do but will provide the specific and valuable business guidance to help you successfully position in the government market.

I am a member of the management consulting industry. I am a small business owner. I am a small business trainer and business coach. I have trained thousands of companies. *But that does not automatically make me a strong consultant.* Doing my job well requires that I understand both federal acquisition and advanced business strategy. From a metrics perspective, my success as a business coach is based solely on the number of clients that win government contracts. That is the *only* metric for my success.

Make sure that when you hire a coach or consultant that you focus on the results that individual has achieved for other / similar companies.

In every industry and profession, there are professionals that do a good job and those that do not. This includes paid consultants. It includes companies' you team with. It includes small business counselors in a myriad of non-profit and for-profit organizations and it includes government employees. There are thousands of consultants and hundreds of organizations chartered to help you with government sales.

In fact, there are so many resources that many companies become confused. One of the most common complaints I hear from small business owners is that there is entirely too much information. They have been given so many recommendations, from so many sources, that they no longer know which ones to trust. This is not unique to the government market. Every job, industry, and market have this challenge. Another reason why I wrote this book.

That being said, there is one organization *you should start with*. That is the Procurement Technical Assistance Center (PTAC). I have harped on the value of the PTAC throughout this book. They are always your first stop. Not only are their services free (funded by the Department of Defense and your local university), they have a stable of government professionals whose job is to help you understand the market. If you have never sold to the government, you start with the PTAC. They will walk you through what you need to do, help you register with the various government systems, and provide the guidance you need to step into government sales.

My team is one of the various resources you have at your fingertips. But the first question I ask every company that calls is whether or not they have engaged their local PTAC. If not, *I immediately recommend they talk to them.*

When you're ready for highly tailored and dedicated support, you may want to consider a business coach or consultant. We will discuss how to not get swindled in the next chapter.

There are tens of thousands of paid and free consultants and counselors across hundreds of organizations. Some are good at what they do. Others are simply a waste of time and money.

Make sure you're asking the right questions.

Something to think about.

Chapter 36.
Before You Hire a Coach or Consultant

There is nothing more frustrating than talking to a company and they tell me they spent $5,000 or $10,000 for a consultant to help them with government sales... and it was a complete waste of money.

They got suckered by a con-artist or they hired someone that was not really an expert. It happens all the time.

I have not had a single client over the last ten years that has not admitted to having had an awful experience with a consultant.

Almost every company has a consultant, is in the process of getting one, or will get one.

So, let's talk about how you make sure you are getting someone that will truly help you.

First, you need referrals. No less than three. Optimum is six. *Talk to every single one.* If it is a reputable company and they have a strong track record, this should be easy. My company has no less than 20 former and current clients that have given us approval to use them for unlimited referrals. So, when someone asks, "Can I get several referrals?" you get the list within a day.

If getting referrals seems to be a challenge, something is wrong. One of the more common responses I have heard is:

"Well, we work with so many companies that protecting the number of times we use a referral is important to us. So how about I give you one or two referrals so I can protect the number of times I go to them?"

Business coaches and consultants that help their clients win contracts are *loved by their clients*. Their clients will do *anything* for them. When I ask past and current clients if they were willing to be referrals on an unlimited basis, almost every single one says, "absolutely!"

So be cautious of consultants that are trying to "protect" the number of times they use referrals. That is a red flag.

Second, do you have the time to focus on improving your company? You need to ask yourself this question and answer it honestly. My team and I have successfully helped hundreds of companies and there are always a few that want to make more money but not take the time to execute the required strategies. In other words, these companies are working IN their business but not ON their business.

So, before you hire a business coach or consultant, make sure you are ready to spend time *on* your business.

Third, set realistic expectations. Regardless of market (commercial or government); regardless of whether you sell products or services, you need to set your expectations at between 12 and 18 months for return on investment (ROI).

Yes, I have helped companies win product contracts in seven days. But even for product companies, you should align your expectations at a year because product sales can run through a dozen different acquisition methods. It may take time to build up your sales.

This does not mean you have to hire a coach or consultant for the entire year. It may just be three or six months. What is important is that you set accurate expectations for yourself. This can be difficult if you are having cash-flow issues.

If you set accurate expectations, then when you win a contract in 6 months, you will be even more excited. You will be less stressed. It is not magic. It is having the right information at the right time with the right business strategy. Give yourself accurate expectations.

Fourth, *don't let the consultant confuse you with other services.*

This is critically important.

The consultant either has the expertise you need or they don't. If you need help getting a GSA Schedule, your *only* focus should be getting a schedule.

Many GSA schedule application companies will say they are experts at government sales and business development - which many of them are not. Sure, a select few have this expertise. I have been in the government market for over 30 years. I have seen quite a bit. Most consultants that are strong at business development and strategy will market themselves as a management consulting or coaching firm. (I refer to myself and my team as executive coaches that specialize in government sales.)

Many GSA schedule application companies will bundle consulting services with their GSA application service in order *to achieve a recurring revenue stream.* If you are going to hire a consultant, they had better be *very good* at what they do.

If you find a GSA schedule application company that appears to also have a very strong management consulting practice, **then ask for two sets of referrals**. Get one for processing GSA schedules and another list of referrals specific to business development and sales.

Two Sets of Referrals
This keeps the consultant from bundling weaker capabilities with their core services.

This helps you when it's time to call their referrals and before you sign an agreement.

You may be told that in addition to whatever they are selling you that, "… at no additional cost, you will be given access to other companies you can team with." Do not let the consultant redirect or confuse you with other services.

From a pure business perspective, if you simply learn the basics of teaming and how to use the federal procurement data system (FPDS) / SAM and other government systems, you do not need those services! If you are performing the right business development activities, you are meeting more companies than you have time to engage! This is a good problem to have!

You should also join a local or national association or coalition for government contractors in your community. For example, if you are a veteran-owned company, you should be a member of the National Veterans Small Business Coalition (NVSBC). It is run by Scott Denniston, the former

Director of Small Business for the Department of Veterans Affairs. If your industry is architecture, engineering, and construction, you should be a member of the Society of American Military Engineers (SAME). If your industry is information technology, cyber security, etc. - you should be a member of the Armed Forces Communications and Electronics Association (AFCEA). There are others. I just happened to list several of the organizations I support.

Bottom line, every consulting firm has additional services that provide value. The question is whether you are paying for what you really need?

Listen to what the consultant has to offer, but make them focus on the challenges you want resolved. Do not let them confuse or *redirect* you with other services.

Fifth, evaluate their website for a sense of their credibility. In today's day and age, it is pretty easy to create a website with whatever message you want to convey. But, for whatever reason, most con-artists and weaker consultants do not spend the time, energy, or have the money to develop a strong website.

I cannot tell you how many websites I have seen that do not list anything about who runs the company! *There are no names.* The site explains how incredible they are and how the value they provide is incredibly awesome, and how incredibly rich you are going to get. Their website has six generic testimonials (no names so you cannot verify) and you have no idea who is actually running the company.

Why would you possibly work with a consultant that does not have their name on their website?

This often happens when the consultant has created multiple companies as a result of the Better Business Bureau getting flooded with complaints. There are always exceptions but this is a common cause.

Do you know any business professionals that own a company that do not 'brand' themselves? For most business owners, it is a sense of pride. Look at me! I own a company! It is basic human nature. It is pride. It is good business. It is smart marketing. It allows potential clients to perform due diligence before they engage.

If the website looks a little too generic and you cannot tell who runs the company or how large the company is – *that is a major red flag*.

If you see their name listed with a short bio but there are no *real testimonials* or market feedback, with some serious teeth to it - that's a red flag too.

Sixth, work with consultants that charge you via a project-based, fixed-price monthly retainer.

In general, I recommend against hiring consultants that charge hourly. There are obvious exceptions, such as your attorney or your CPA. But that's not the type of consultant we are talking about. I know this flies in the face of many consultants in the market, but if you think about this logically, it makes sense.

My company does not charge hourly. We have several coaching and consulting levels that all have a fixed monthly rate. Why? Because every company is different. Every company has unique requirements and it is way too easy for you to hear, "Sorry, that is not included in the scope of work I am providing you."

Sure, companies take advantage of project-based / fixed-rate retainers, but if the right expectations are set, it should not be an issue. Once or twice a month I am asked to perform several hours of work (from companies we don't currently support) and I'll set a price. For example, one of our clients asked for a complete propensity breakdown for fifteen companies. They wanted to know how much each company sold, to which agencies, for how much, who their teaming partners were, and another dozen data points. They knew how to do it, but were crashing on a proposal and needed some extra help. Yes, in those situations, I will work hourly and charge for it.

A project-based or fixed-price retainer lets you know exactly what you are paying for every month with the peace of mind that you will get what you need. Focus on the *statement of work* and make sure you understand what is and is not covered.

You also have to be realistic with your consultant or coach. As coaches, we know that companies will push as far and as fast as they can to get as much as they can. Nothing wrong with this. This is normal. It's business. But a project-based retainer needs to be mutually beneficial.

Find the right consultant that operates with fixed monthly rates, with strong referrals, and you are on the right path to finding some quality help.

And that brings us to **Number 7** - The Better Business Bureau (BBB). This is so easy to check but I am going to make several points.

First, not every company has a history with the Better Business Bureau. For example, my company is not registered with the BBB. Why? Because it never came up when we opened our doors and there has never been a need to do it. Maybe one day, but there is so much information about RSM Federal online that we never felt it was necessary. We rely on the hundreds of testimonials on our website for due-diligence.

So, if the consultant's company is not listed with the BBB, it just means you have to do some additional due diligence. I would check ripoffreport.com to make sure there are not any negative remarks or comments.

There are many consulting firms, both commercial and government, that are listed with the Better Business Bureau. Here is another common question: How many complaints make the company a risk? That raises a red flag? In my opinion, the answer is two or more. Some people game the system and use the Internet to launch attacks on reputable businesses.

But if you are ethical and you know how to run your company and set accurate expectations with your clients, complaints to the Better Business Bureau *should not happen*.

Sometimes they do. But in the world of government business coaches and consultants, it is very rare if you are taking care of your clients and setting accurate expectations.

I have seen government consulting firms with more than 30 complaints. So what if they were all resolved? So what if the consulting firm refunded the money? If you are properly setting expectations with your clients and both sides understand the statement of work, you have to be pretty screwed-up, unethical, or a con-artist to get so many complaints.

If you have thousands of clients buying your services, I still do not buy the excuse that 30 complaints should be expected and is simply the price of doing business. That is just too many red flags for me. That is just too much uncertainty. *What if I become one of those 30? Is that just the price of doing business?*

That consulting firm is average, at best. That many complaints are a pattern of non-compliance.

So, get at least three referrals (six is better!) and talk to them in detail.

Make sure you have the time to work with your consultant.

Set accurate expectations for yourself on how quickly a consultant can realistically do what they say they can do.

Do not let a consultant confuse you and redirect you with other services (*that they think will get you to sign their contract.*)

And check their website for management information and Google them online and check the Better Business Bureau for complaints.

Whether or not you know the consultant, you *must* trust them.

How do you trust someone you don't know? You take these 7 recommendations into account.

Something to think about.

Chapter 37.
You Can't Afford a Business Developer?

Okay, you want to grow your company? You need someone to review opportunities and identify which ones you are going to bid on. You want a hunter! You want a business developer that will take your company to the next level. If you didn't know, the best business developers on the market will double your company's revenue in one year.

In your mind, **you might as well be looking for a unicorn**.

For the purpose of this chapter, a unicorn is that mythical sales creature that everyone has except you. Other companies have unicorns, but not your company.

I know. You cannot afford to hire a strong business developer.

… or so you think.

Many companies walk through a mental process that goes something like this:

"Do I have to hire them? Can I 1099 them? If I 1099 them, then I don't have to worry about healthcare, laptop, and other benefits. If I could just win one more contract, I could afford a sales person. Oh! You know what? I will just find some hungry millennial or a semi-retired sales person to work commission only."

Yes, you can hire them. You can 1099 them. You can go down that nutty-road of commission-only. You can also outsource your sales to another company. Companies try all of these.

What would I do? Well, it is different for every company.

But I want you to consider several points. First, whether you hire, contract, or outsource, all of these will require the *same level of ramp-up*. In

241

my professional opinion, if I had to rank the speed in which one of these options will win you a contract, it would be:

1) W2 employee

2) 1099 contractor

3) Outsourced (another company)

4) Commission-only

When you outsource, some will provide you with a ton of sales and market data, much of which is free and you can find yourself. (I think there's a system called Federal Access that will teach you how to find market and contract data.)

I do not know the exact percentages, but my experience in the government market has shown that *less than 10% of companies that outsource their business development actually win a contract.*

10%.

That means 9 out of 10 companies that outsource their sales pay a lot of money and never get a contract. Just like outsourcing proposal support, smaller and mid-tier companies may decide that outsourcing business development and sales is their only viable option.

If you are going to outsource, remember what the knight says to Indiana Jones when selecting a chalice for the holy grail . . . "Choose wisely."

Outsourcing your sales is less likely to achieve your objectives.

A strong, qualified, and proven business developer will take three (3) months to understand your company, your products or services, and most important... I will say it again, most important is being able to *market and communicate the value of what you sell.* If you have difficulty communicating the value of your products and services, your business developers will not be able to either.

If you think you are going to outsource your business development to another company, they still have to educate themselves on who you are, what you do, and the value you provide.

Think about it! If it is going to take three months for a W2 employee to learn about your company and solutions and how to position them in the market, why would it be any different for a company you outsource to? Thinking logically, it should take the company you have outsourced even longer!

There are thousands of consultants and companies that provide business development services. Very few of them actually do what they say they can. I know from experience and from talking with colleagues, that most companies have a story about paying someone for 12 months and they never won a contract.

But, let me go off on another tangent. I believe there are two positions you should never attempt to outsource. They are proposal development and business development. Why? Because even if you win a contract, you have very little of the intellectual capital you just paid someone else to do. Sure, you have a copy of the proposal. But it is *not* the proposal, the template for the proposal, or the content in the proposal that ultimately wins the contract.

It is the *strategy behind how the proposal was written.*

If you think this is semantics or a philosophical point, it is not. You have just generated revenue but there is no increase in the maturity of your business or its processes.

This is one of the most important points I can make. You need to increase both revenue and corporate maturity *in order to grow your company.*

I know, you are focused on cash-flow and you will "worry about growing your maturity" after you have won a big contract. Well, that's great. But many companies still do not feel they have enough cash-flow, even after winning a contract. Many companies are right back where they started 12 months after the contract is awarded.

So where does that leave us? You may be thinking, "come on Josh! I cannot afford a sales person right now. But I can afford a couple thousand dollars a month for one of these companies to do it for me." Or, just as likely, you may be thinking, "I will hire a sales person commission only."

Yes, there are companies that successfully help other companies with business development. I have relationships with a couple of them. But your odds of finding the right company are 1 in a 100. Do you like those odds? Remember, hope is not a strategy.

You can increase your odds by 10% if you spend a couple months talking to colleagues and doing some hardcore due diligence. But it is still just a one in ten chance of success.

If there was a great answer for outsourcing, everyone would be doing it and we would not have so many business owners complaining about the money they wasted.

There are also many companies (small and large) that look for commission-only business developers.

Yes, thousands of companies, especially small businesses, try to find commission-only sales people. *You should NOT consider this option.*

I have had this discussion with hundreds of companies. There are very few 'good business developers' that will work commission only. Why? Because if they are good at winning contracts, someone has *already hired them*.

I do not know any strong business developers that work commission only.

None.

Zero.

They are too good at what they do. They are not going to work without a base salary.

What that means is that the majority of sales people that are willing to work on commission are either making money with another company (and that is where their focus lies), or they are doing commission only while looking for another job.

Let me say this again - you are *highly unlikely* to find a decent business developer without both a base salary and a commission structure.

So where does that leave you?

You have several options. First, look at your expenses and cut back so you can afford to hire a business developer.

Maybe you are leasing office space. Do you really need the back-half of your office? Give it back and you can expand once you have generated more revenue.

That annual vacation you take every year to the Caribbean? That is two months' salary for a business developer.

That Mercedes you are getting ready to buy? Buy a car that is half the cost.

Do you really need to exhibit at those three conferences? Ask yourself how much revenue you made last year as a result of those conferences? Do not answer this with a guess. *Show me* the metrics where you can cross-walk contracts you have won as a *direct or indirect result* of attending a conference.

If you cannot directly attribute revenue to any of those conferences, why are you spending the money again this year? Perhaps you should only exhibit at one or two. Maybe you do not have to exhibit at any of them and you should just attend and 'work' the exhibit hall. You have just saved another two months of a business developer's salary.

You may have to make some hard decisions that will impact your quality of life until you win one or two more contracts.

Couple other thoughts. If you hire a full-time employee, they are going to act like a member of your team. If you hire a contractor, no matter how hard they work for you, they do not have the same perceptions or feelings as a full-time employee. They are simply a contractor. There are many business professionals that make a living as a contractor. We are not talking about contractors on government contracts. We are talking about a 1099 business developer. Are you giving them health benefits? Probably not. They are not going to look at your company the same way as an employee.

Another option is to do it yourself like when you first started your company. Evaluate all the activities you are doing and make a note next to each. Identify which activities directly produce revenue and which ones do not. You may find a large percentage of your activities are focused on more strategic outcomes. If I was your business coach, 6 times out of 10, the companies I work with are equally focused on their brand as they are revenue. Build your brand, identify your message, and put it to bed! Then spend your time on sales.

Here is what I know for sure. A large number of companies spend one or more years contracting or outsourcing business development and the company never grows. More times than not, the new contracts came from the owner or senior manager, not the business developers you outsourced.

Even if your revenue this year will be $1.4 million, you may need to go back to working those crazy hours you had hoped were behind you.

By now it should be clear that outsourcing your business development is, oftentimes, not in your best interest. Yes, there are some awesome companies that you can pay to do it for you, but most of them will not work out. If you decide to outsource, you need to mitigate your risk by calling every referral they give you and then doing even more research on their past performance.

A full-time employee will be more likely to win a contract than a 1099 contractor.

But you are still thinking, "Yea Josh, I get it. But I still cannot afford to hire someone as an employee."

You are wrong. *You can*. You can afford the best and the brightest with an average to above average salary and a killer commission plan that has commission escalators. If they bring-in $2 million in contracts, they receive a 2% commission. Between $2.1 million and $3 million, they get 3% in commissions. If they win more contracts and exceed $3.1 million in sales, they get 4% in commissions.

In this example, let's assume that $65,000 is an average salary in your region. Your new business developer's sales quota is $2 million. You hire them and six months later they win three contracts worth $2 million. At 2% they just made $40,000 in commissions. But then they exceed your wildest dreams and close another contract for another $1 million. Because they exceeded their annual sales quota, the escalator for this contract is 3%. So, they just made another $30,000. If they do not win any more contracts, they closed $3 million in new business. Assuming your margins are in the 5% to 20% range, your company is making good money!

Let's assume your margin on these contracts was 12%. Your company just made $360,000 in profit. Your business developer? They just made $135,000 in total compensation (base + commissions). So instead of making $360,000, your company is making $225,000 in profit.

Imagine if your margins were 18%? Your company would be making $405,000 in profit.

Any company can afford to hire the markets top talent. You simply need a strong compensation plan!

I have heard many business owners say, "There is no way I am paying *some sales person* $350,000 a year. That is ridiculous! That is more than I pay myself and I'm the owner!"

If this is you, you need to decide if growing your company is a priority. I often respond with, "Why are you stuck on this? Yes, you may pay an employee more than you pay yourself, *but it is your company*. Your company may have just made $1.2 million in profit and that is after you paid your business developer $350,000!

How do you afford the best and the brightest? You build a compensation package that allows them to **make more money than anyone else in your company**.

I've written several articles on building compensation packages. There is a phenomenal white-paper, with step-by-step strategies and examples that you can download in the Federal Access Knowledge-Base.

So, which option is most likely to get you where you want to be? Hire, 1099, outsource, or do it yourself until you win the next contract?

Build a compensation package, hire the strongest business developer you can find, and double your company's revenue.

Who cares if your business developer is making more money than the owner of the company?

If you are a business owner, think like a business owner.

Something to think about.

Chapter 38.
How to Interview Your Next Business Developer

This is an excellent transition from the last chapter! What are your expectations for a new business developer? How long should it take for a new business developer to win their first government contract?

If you already have one or more business developers and they are not winning contracts, review the concepts and strategies that we discussed in Chapter 10, *Walking Opportunities Through Your Pipeline*. I also recorded a podcast on "Why Business Developers Fail and What To Do About It." It's free. Just head over to the Podcast Game Changers for Government Contractors on either iTunes or Soundcloud.

The 3-6-12 Month Business Development Cycle

For this chapter, we are going to assume that you have decided to hire a full-time business developer. If not, you still need to understand these concepts because one day you'll need them.

Let's discuss perceptions and expectations when you are interviewing your next sales person. In general, we know that the sales-cycle for government sales can be longer than commercial sales. Where a commercial sale may take 7-10 touches, it can take 10-20 for government contracts.

One of the more common challenges facing small and mid-tier companies are the expectations on when a new business developer should bring in their first contract. For product or commodity sales, the first contract could be a matter of weeks. That is the power of using DLAs Internet Bid Board System (DIBBS) and other government systems. If you sell services, many business owners believe their new business developer should close a contract in 3 to 6 months.

This is not a viable expectation for selling services in the government market.

To help you think about this logically, let me tell you about the last time I interviewed for a job. It was for a sales position in a small business that was also woman-owned and 8(a) minority-owned. For the purpose of this discussion, the size and socio-economic status is irrelevant.

The company flew its vice president to Washington D.C. to interview me. I was then asked to fly to the Midwest to sit down with the owner. The owner asked me a fairly standard question, "How long will it take for you to win a contract?"

My answer was 12 to 14 months. At least a year. The owner just looked at me. No one spoke for thirty seconds. I am sure she was thinking, *'why did I just agree to fly him in*? And what the heck is wrong with my vice president for recommending this guy?'

Everyone else they had interviewed had responded with three to six months because most business developers do not want to say it will take a year. This assumes they understand how long it takes to win a contract.

I am also sure the owner was thinking, *"Why would I ever consider hiring a business developer that will not pay for themselves for an entire year?"*

Instead, she was smart and she asked a question that every company, *your company*, needs to ask: "Can you outline how you position in the market, identify opportunities, engage those opportunities, position with both the government and teaming partners, and how you work with the proposal writers to ensure we have the necessary intelligence to win a contract?"

Beautiful.

In other words, *"What strategies do you use and explain how you engage and move opportunities through the pipeline?"* If you are jumping from chapter to chapter, you may want to go back and read the Chapter 10 on *Walking Opportunities Through Your Pipeline*.

This question is *much more important* than calling their past references. It is much more important than asking how successful they were at their last company. *Anyone* can influence their references and anyone can fudge their past success.

Consider all the resumes you have seen.

You know resumes are inflated. You need to focus on the strategies for engaging opportunities, *not their past success.*

Some readers are thinking, "Of course their past performance and success is important. That is a core metric I use for deciding to hire folks."

But how do you really know if they won all those contracts or it was the work of others on their team? So, when the owner asked me this question, here is the first part of my response:

"First, it will take three months to understand the company. Sure, I can figure out what services you sell in a matter of minutes. But to be highly successful, I have to understand the value you provide to your clients.

I have to understand the company's past performance and study each contract to understand the value provided, the level of effort, and how to differentiate the company and its services. Differentiating the company applies not only to government prospects but with teaming partners as well.

*To be successful, I have to map the value of the company's services against the requirements of **every** specific opportunity."*

This is normal for highly skilled sale's professionals. This is how strong sale's professionals operate. This is how you convince teaming partners that you will make them more competitive.

This is how you win contracts.

I continued:

*"So, the first three months are understanding the company, how to differentiate, and how to position in the market. During these three months and through the first six months, I start filling the pipeline and positioning for opportunities both as a prime and a subcontractor. The first 6 months are for understanding the company, the value it provides, engaging opportunities and **building a pipeline**.*

*Then months 6 through 12, I am meeting with various government representatives, attending industry days, meeting with teaming partners, attending one or two conferences, and working the pipeline. Yes, I do much of this in the first six months, **but I am up and running, at full speed, in month 6**."*

I looked at the owner and finished with,

"It is not a question of if. It is a question of when. Based on personal experience, I expect to win the first major contract in about a year. I will also have an extensive number of opportunities where we will be well positioned for the following year."

A little after 13 months, I positioned for and won a $10 million subcontract with IBM in support of USTRANSCOM. That was 10 years ago. The company still has this contract. The point of this story is that the 3-6-12 month business development cycle *should be applied to your expectations* in the government market.

If you are a service-based company, anyone that tells you they will close a deal in less time is probably telling you that because they want the job. There is nothing wrong with that. But your expectations should be somewhere around a year. If they close a deal sooner, that's great!

I often tell business owners to set expectations for a year and to plan their cash flow accordingly.

Not all business developers are going to understand the 3-6-12 month business development cycle. Even those that do may still tell you six months. Why not? They want the job.

This is why your focus with candidates should be on their strategy and how they identify and move opportunities through the pipeline. You are focused on how they position with the government and with teaming partners. You need to ask hard questions about how they communicate value and competitive advantage.

You will quickly learn if the business developer you are interviewing knows what they are doing. You either understand how to perform business development or you don't.

We all know that it costs a lot of money to hire the wrong employee. For business developers, focus on their strategies and how they engage and position in the market.

You have no idea if that $8 million contract they just won was because they did the legwork or someone else on their team did.

Do not focus on their past success.

Ask them to walk you through, step-by-step, how they engage the market.

Ask them to outline their process for *walking opportunities through the pipeline*.

Something to think about.

Chapter 39.
Outsourcing Proposal Development

The topic of hiring a proposal writer is probably one of the top five challenges that we discuss with our clients and members.

For proposal development, anyone can write a proposal. Writing a *winning* proposal is another matter. Knowing how to map the value of your products or services to the government's or teaming partner's requirements is a greater challenge.

You need to have an intrinsic understanding of the company, the products and services, and how to differentiate and communicate competitive advantage. You need this when you map your value to the government or teaming partner's requirements.

If you outsource proposal development, yes, you may win a contract, but you will not have the intellectual capital of how it was done. There are some very good consultants that will help you write proposals and some of them will win.

I referred to this in a previous chapter. A company's growth is often dependent on *internal maturity and capability*. While you may not be able to afford a quality proposal writer or proposal manager, it is in your best interest to hire one as soon as cash-flow allows.

Every time a large Government Wide Acquisition Contract (GWAC), an Indefinite Delivery Indefinite Quantity (IDIQ) contract, or a Multiple Award Task Order Contract (MATOC) is released for competition, you receive one or more emails from companies and proposal support firms offering to write the proposal for you.

To be clear, there are some very good proposal development companies. In my opinion, there are very few that are really good at writing competitive proposals. Of those that have the business acumen to write a truly competitive proposal, only a small percentage are at prices that small businesses can afford. This is why most proposal development companies target mid-tier and large businesses. Small businesses can rarely afford these services.

Of course, the next question is how much do these services cost? There is no right answer. It depends on the company providing the service. It depends on the size of the proposal.

On average, outsourcing a twenty to thirty-page proposal will cost you between $2,000 and $10,000. I am familiar with a dozen companies that paid $50,000 to $100,000 for a proposal. Each of the proposals was for a large IDIQ where the maximum number of contracts awarded was twenty or less awardees.

Of the twelve that paid this much money, six won. Considering average industry win-rates, 50% is not bad. You have to spend money to make money. But $100,000 for a losing bid is a lot of money.

Writing a winning proposal also assumes that the proposal firm understands your company, understands what you sell, your past performance, the value of your products and services, your strengths and weaknesses, the strengths and weaknesses of your competition, and how to properly differentiate and communicate competitive advantage.

If a proposal firm can do all these things (in a very short period of time), they are absolutely worth the money. But finding one of these firms is *highly difficult*. There are thousands of companies that can help you write a good proposal.

But *good* proposals do not win contracts.

Based on my experience, companies that successfully outsource proposal development have two common attributes. First, they have won a contract in the last twelve months (have the cash-flow to afford the cost of outsourced proposal development) and second, their proposal team is under-water.

Often times, these services are targeting companies where the proposal writer or team is so busy that the company needs an extra resource, another hand, to help write another proposal.

Absolutely nothing wrong with outsourced proposal development services if it is the right decision at the right time for your company.

If you are one of those companies that can afford $2,000 to $10,000 to outsource a proposal, I have a couple of close colleagues that I can recommend. But I will not recommend anyone unless I'm convinced it is in your best interest. Yea, I'm hard-core.

Due to most small businesses being unable to afford these services, many proposal firms have created another solution. They will sell you the "outline" you can use to write your proposal. I have seen many of these and some of them are quite good. If you know how to review an RFP and create a proposal template, it is not hard to generate an outline. The hard part is writing the proposal itself. On average, these outlines run between $75 and $500.

But here is what makes me scratch my head. I want you to think about this from a business perspective. If you know how to review an RFP, identify and list all the requirements and you know how to set-up your proposal, you probably do not need to pay for an outline.

If you need an outline, chances are you probably do not understand how to organize and *write a winning the proposal*.

So, for many smaller businesses, based on this logic, buying the proposal outline implies they will have challenges writing a competitive proposal.

Buying an outline will help them better understand how to review an RFP and better understand how to map the requirements within their response. So, buying these outlines is not a cut and dry decision. If you are still learning how to write a strong proposal, I have no problem recommending the use of outlines.

Remember, government contracting is a long-game. It takes education, time, and experience. As part of that education and experience, one of the best ways to learn how to write a proposal is to *be on another company's team*. This way you get to watch, listen, and learn how other companies do it.

90% of small businesses win their first several contracts as a subcontractor. Knowing this to be the case, you should join several teams, watch how they manage the proposal process and grab a copy of the proposal so you can learn from it.

Also remember that a strong teaming strategy will increase the number of opportunities in your pipeline by 400%. If you have won some contracts, your proposal team is swamped, and you need to outsource a proposal effort, just make sure you get referrals.

Every company is different. But at the end of the day, it comes down to understanding what is best for your company.

Something to think about.

Chapter 40.
Generic Emails To 'Join A Team'

When you have been in the System for Award Management (SAM) for any period of time, you will start receiving generic emails from companies that are building teams for major government procurements. 95% of these emails will be *after* the RFP or RFQ has been released.

For companies new to government sales, these emails can be very, very appealing. "Look! I didn't even know about this opportunity!" or "I never thought we would find a team and now we have a chance."

From a business perspective, let's discuss the ramifications of this scenario.

Let's use the Department of Veterans Affairs VECTOR Contract as an example. VECTOR is a massive multiple award task order contract (MATOC). It is a ten-year, $25 billion contract. The Department of Veterans Affairs awarded contracts to 68 teams. Assuming the average team consists of at least five companies, there are more than 340 companies competing for $25 billion in task order contracts. There are probably many more companies on these teams.

My company is on one of these teams and our team has almost twenty companies. Why so many companies? Because it took that many to be competitive; because the prime (Technical Assent) had companies with strong past performance in *every task area*. I discuss this concept on teaming to maximize coverage on all task areas in the Chapter 22 – *Failure to Team. Failure to Win.*

Continuing with this example, if your company has a solid sales strategy and the Department of Veterans Affairs is one of your annual targets, then you probably knew about the VECTOR acquisition long before it was released on SAM.

Odds are you had already decided to prime or join a team and had already initiated your teaming strategy. You probably had a teaming agreement signed before the RFP was released.

There were thousands of veteran-owned small businesses that had no clue that VECTOR was going to be competed. They saw it for the first time on SAM. Many of these companies read the RFP and said, "Ugh, way too big for us and we don't have a team for it."

And now we come full circle. These are the small businesses that receive those generic emails from 'team-building' companies and wonder if this is their path to winning. The companies that send these generic emails are looking for the less mature businesses that do not have their finger on the pulse of the opportunity.

These team-building companies are also targeting small businesses that have no experience bidding on and writing a 100-page proposal. That is a fair point.

What normally happens is that a company receives an email and they say to themselves:

"Wow, if we don't get on this contract, we will be out in the cold for the next 10 years. It is a veteran set-aside and we spent all that time and money getting VOSB or SDVOSB certified. We have no choice! We have to go after this!"

Well... actually, you do have a choice. You may not like it. For a contract of this magnitude, do you have market intelligence that will make you competitive?

These 'team-building' companies are hoping to take advantage of your excitement, lack of market knowledge, and the belief that you have no choice but to go after it.

Most of the companies that pursued VECTOR as a prime knew about the acquisition six months to a year before it was released publicly. Many heard about it at the National Veterans Small Business Engagement (NVSBE) conference the year before (another reason why you need to pick the right government conferences to attend.)

If you want to prime and the first time you heard about a VECTOR type contract was after the RFP was released, you are probably not going to win. You have not had time to collect intelligence or write a draft proposal. You are also unlikely to find subcontractors that will make your team highly competitive. Why? Because those companies have already been snatched-up by other primes.

My point is that these generic emails about joining a team has gone out to several thousand companies. Sometimes they win. Most times they do not.

Bottom line. If you want to prime one of these large IDIQ or MATOC contracts, to be competitive, you need to be aware of the opportunity *before the RFP is released.*

If the first time you hear about an opportunity is after the RFP is released, whether you want to prime or subcontract, remember that most of the other teams have already been established. Many of the teams have already started their proposals.

So, what should you do if you first see the opportunity on SAM? You should try to find an existing team *that you believe will be competitive.* Then convince them that your company will make the overall team more competitive.

Hope is not a strategy.

You have to understand market dynamics.

You need to have a strong teaming strategy as part of your overall business development strategy.

You need to focus on pre-acquisition activities, build relationships with your government targets, and collect market intelligence.

Something to think about.

Chapter 41.
Saving Money on Government Conferences

I f you sell to the government, you probably attend two or three conferences every year. They may be local, regional, or national events.

I was on a monthly strategy call with one of our Federal Access members and they asked:

"Josh, you support a dozen national events every year. Do you have any recommendations on how to better plan for them and protect our costs?"

What a great question because we always focus on what to do before you arrive and what you should do once you get there, but not tricks on the financial aspects. So, here are a couple of financial strategies I use when planning to attend a conference.

First, there are always a large number of folks who do not register or coordinate travel until a week or two before the conference. Often times this is the result of not knowing if they will be able to attend.

If you are like many companies, you have other requirements and it is difficult to know if you will be free to go.

This is a perfect case of not seeing the forest through the trees.

If you wait until the last minute, you are going to pay 20% more on registration, 40% more on airfare, and the conference hotel will be sold out.

Of these three (registration, airfare, and hotel), the **hotel is the most important**. Sure, you will pay an extra $200 for registration and an extra $350 for airfare, but that combined $550 is nothing compared *to not being at the conference hotel and venue.*

Many think, "I don't need to stay at the conference hotel. I'll just be down the block and I'll walk."

Staying at the primary hotel, the hotel linked to the conference center, allows you to stay at the conference center longer each night; allows you to get up later in the morning so you are more refreshed; allows you more time to 'bump' into key people you want to partner with; and many of the evening events, held by other contractors, are in the primary hotel.

So, I want to provide some recommendations and when I give them, you are going to say, "duh, I knew that." But then you are going to make a note and actually do some of them.

In late December, I put a piece of paper on the wall and I map out all the conferences I plan to attend. I put them in a timeline so I can see month to month where I want or need to go.

Then I put each conference or event onto my Outlook calendar. If I am not sure I will be able to go, then I mark it as tentative in the calendar. This way, I can quickly scroll through the calendar and see which events are confirmed and which are tentative.

Back to the paper timeline on my wall. I write four checkboxes under each event: airfare, hotel, rental car, and registration. (I will also add exhibit if I plan to exhibit). This allows me to quickly look-up and see what is coordinated or not coordinated for every event.

Most conferences have their websites updated early in the year. One of the first things I do in January is reserve a room for every conference. I will even do this for conferences in December the following year. Why not? I can cancel any of them within 24 hours of the conference. Even if I cannot go, I am not losing any money. Most important, for *every* conference I attend I will be at the primary hotel attached to the conference.

Yes, you have to make sure you have a process to review your reservations so you do not get charged for a room you did not use. But that is easy. Just make sure it is on your calendar.

Second, depending on your airline, you can often cancel airfare and 100% of the funds are available for a future ticket. This is one of the reasons I fly Southwest every chance I get. Yes, I'm a Southwest snob.

I make airline reservations between three and four months prior to the event. For events I want to attend, I will know 80% of the time if I will be attending four months before the conference.

Every year, there are one or two events where something prevents me from going. But over the last 10 years, I have *never lost a single penny*. I just transfer those funds to another flight in the next 12 months.

So even if I decide not to attend a conference, I just cancel my hotel and recoup the airfare. By doing it this way, I am guaranteed decent airfare and primary hotel.

When it comes to rental cars, my decision on whether or not to get one depends on the number of employees going with me. If I am going alone, 9 times out of 10 a cab (or Uber) is just as expensive or less expensive as a rental car. Don't forget to take into account that $25 a night parking fee at the hotel or the $20 in gas.

If there are two or more people, it might make more sense to get a rental car.

Either way, you can do your rental car a week before the trip. That is easy.

For the final coordination point, I mark on my timeline when early registration ends for each conference and I make sure it is on my calendar. Often times, early registration is good until a month or two prior to the event.

Bottom line, there are a lot of business professionals that treat conferences as unimportant and a last-minute requirement.

It does not take a lot of time to do what I do. You are already looking at which conferences you want to attend. Write them down, add checkboxes for airfare, hotel, rental car, and registration. Then spend 30 minutes making your hotel reservations.

Many companies do not take advantage of conferences and when they do attend, they are so scattered, stressed, or mentally exhausted that they do not achieve the value that they should.

Do some simple planning. It will save you time, money, and make each event more beneficial.

So, which conferences are you attending this year? Once you have them identified, put some paper on the wall and map them out.

Something to think about.

Chapter 42.
Celebrate Your Small Successes

T his is one of the most important business lessons I have learned in my professional career.

For more than five years, I supported a company in Bakersfield, California called Tel-Tec Security. I helped Tel-Tec win their first 13 contracts. The owner of the company is a man by the name of Morgan Clayton. He has been running Tel-Tec for more than 40 years.

He is also one of the nicest individuals I have ever had the privilege to work with. He has a highly successful security business. But what sets him apart is his focus on helping others.

I flew to California and early one morning we were having breakfast and he asked about my business and family. I told him that I was working fast and furious, that I was racing from one requirement to another and that I was very busy.

He then asked me a question that changed my mental outlook, something that seems so small and trivial but made a massive difference in how I approach both my personal and professional life.

He asked, *"Do you celebrate your small successes?"*

I responded with, "Of course I do. Every now and then I'll take my wife out to a nice restaurant when the company gets new business."

Morgan looked at me and smiled. He said: "That is not enough. You do not want to simply celebrate your successes … you need to celebrate the small successes. It is what keeps you mentally healthy. It is what keeps you pumped and excited about your job."

I tilted my head to the side and asked him to explain.

He asked: "Do you celebrate when you are asked to keynote a government conference? Do you celebrate when you have completed a proposal and turned it in or only after you have won the contract?

Do you celebrate when you have had an awesome sales call with a new prospect or only after that prospect has signed a contract with your company?

Bottom line, when something good happens, do you take the time to step back, take a breath, and admit to yourself that you have done a good job?"

"Success is not simply defined as making money. You need to constantly remind yourself to step back, take a breath, and congratulate yourself for doing your job well."

That simple discussion over breakfast changed how I approach business. It changed how I run my company. It gave me a different mental outlook. Granted, I sometimes forget and have to remind myself. Nowadays, I force myself to read this chapter!

I like cigars. I have a humidor. Yes, I know, many of you think they are nasty. Hey! We all have our vices. Even though I love cigars, I only smoke a couple a month. I will not give you trouble about your vices. For those that smoke cigars and are wondering what I smoke (this is a cigar thing), I prefer Dominican Fuente Gran Reserva 858 and my two favorites 'sticks' are Cuban Partagas and Bolivar.

If I work my butt-off, presented a great webinar, sent out several agreements, and kept really focused during the week, I will remind myself that I am doing the right activities. In these situations, I will take a walk in the park and smoke a cigar. It gets me out of the office!

I even have a sign on the wall, with a picture of a cigar, to remind me to enjoy the small successes.

What about you? Other than when you win contracts or sign new clients, do you ever step back and take a breath? Do you go outside, take a walk, and think about how well you just performed a requirement or an activity?

It is not simply about making money.

If you celebrate your small successes, you will find that life becomes just a little less stressful and a lot more fulfilling.

Something to think about.

Chapter 43.
Government Sales Is Stressing Me Out!

I n all reality, *the market you are selling to is immaterial*. Whether it is commercial or government sales - winning business, making payroll, and covering your costs are always going to be stressful. That is the life of a business owner or business professional.

We are always talking about winning the next contract. For this chapter, let's take a moment to shift our focus from 'how to win' to 'how do you deal with the uncertainty?' In other words, the grind, the stress of pursuing new contracts.

Do You Have a Mentor?
And off we go on another tangent. Throughout my business career, I have always had a mentor – even today! Another difference between a job and an occupation is having a mentor. If you don't have one, get one.

In 2005, I worked for an amazing boss. His name was Dan Ragheb. Dan passed away several years ago but he was instrumental in helping make me the business professional I am today.

I was managing the Department of Defense for MasterCard Worldwide in Washington D.C. We were coordinating and building relationships with all of the large banking institutions. They included Bank of America, Citigroup, US Bank, Melon Bank, and several others.

I was responsible for facilitating partnerships between MasterCard and the banks for a government program. If you have been selling to the government for even several months, you have probably heard of it. It is called the General Service Administration's (GSA) SmartPay program. It is where federal agencies and the armed services use credit cards to make small purchases.

Still not familiar? This is the program that supports *micro-purchases*. It is the program where all federal agencies and the military services get their credit cards. The micro-purchase threshold for federal agencies and the Department of Defense is $10,000. The threshold has increased three times in the last several years. It will probably continue to increase as the government continues to improve its acquisition strategies.

Working for MasterCard required an indirect sales model. While I spoke with all of the program offices across all the military services, the final decision to use MasterCard would be outside my direct control. The decision would be between the banks and the military services, *not MasterCard*.

Getting the banks to select MasterCard over Visa was a *multi-billion-dollar* decision.

Dan and I knew that Visa had the upper hand. They were promising larger rebates; had stronger online tools; and most important, they had stronger relationships with the Department of Defense and the federal agencies.

Trying to position MasterCard's solutions over Visa's was stressing me out. I was the de-facto Business Leader at MasterCard for the Department of Defense.

I was stressed. Dan saw it and he pulled me aside one afternoon. Similar to the advice Morgan Clayton gave me on 'celebrating your smaller successes,' Dan also gave me life-changing advice. He handed me a book. It was written by Dale Carnegie called *How to Stop Worrying and Start Living.*" NOTE [27]

If you have not read this book, I highly recommend it. The overall summary is that ninety percent of everything you worry about... during

---

[27] How to Stop Worrying and Start Living, Gallery Books; Revised edition (October 5, 2004), https://www.amazon.com/gp/product/0671035975 ISBN-13: 978-0671035976,

your entire lifetime... *will never happen*. Ninety percent of what keeps you up at night will never come to pass.

Carnegie interviewed thousands of business professionals from all walks of life. Now, you may be wondering, "Where am I going with this?"

Well, Carnegie said that anytime you are worried about something, you need to ask yourself one question:

"What is the worst thing that can happen?"

Think about the things that keep you up at night. It might be writing a proposal for an opportunity you know you can win. It could be hiring a new business developer that is critical to your future success. How about that meeting with a new government prospect? Perhaps it is a meeting with a program manager that you spent six months cultivating?

This is not simply a philosophical concept. I want you to ask yourself, out loud, "what is the worst thing that could happen?"

If you are writing a proposal and you are hoping to win because your company needs a new contract, what is the worst thing that can happen?

The worst thing? You don't win the contract.

Carnegie says that after you identify the worst thing that can happen, that you **simply accept it**. There is something about identifying the worst and then mentally accepting it... that changes your perception and puts you in a different frame of mind.

I may not do it consciously, but I do it every day.

So whatever stresses you have at work, ask yourself, out loud, "what's the worst thing that can happen?"

Then mentally accept it.

It will change your mental outlook and alleviate some of the stress. If you have not read his book, I would argue it is just as important as all those sales books you have on your bookshelf.

Something to think about.

271

Chapter 44.
Travelling in Comfort

This chapter is a bit less cerebral. It is about business travel. There is nothing worse than arriving at your destination and forgetting something back at the office.

I remember exhibiting at the Defense Information Systems Agency's (DISA) annual conference (when DISA had an annual conference), and I forgot to pack the marketing collateral for our booth.

I remember flying to Washington D.C for a meeting with Health and Human Services (HHS) and not only did I forget my briefing, I forgot the thumb-drive.

Probably the most annoying mistake was forgetting to pack the power cord to my laptop for a conference in Texas. My laptop was to be the primary display for the trade-show booth. My wife is an absolute saint. She shipped the power cord overnight to my hotel. If you have ever had to do this, it is not as easy as it sounds. It is a royal pain in the butt. It's also very expensive. You can be sure that I never did that again!

Jump forward to this revised edition of this book. The last sentence above? *You can be sure I never did that again*? Right... just two months ago I supported the state of Texas' Veterans conference and guess what I left in the hotel seminar room? Uh-huh. My laptop power cord. I called Earl Morgan, the Program Director for the National Veteran Small Business Coalition (NVSBC) and one of the most awesome guys I've ever met, and begged him to find my power cord and ship it back to my office. There is nothing that has ever stopped Earl. I had my power cord back in less than a week. Oh! And he shipped two toys for my kids! Just an awesome human being.

Wait a minute.

I just realized, as I was updating this chapter, that BOTH times I've had a problem with my power cord... *it was in Texas.*

A = B

B = C

Therefore A = C

I'm never going back to Texas.

Back to the first time I forgot my power cord. So instead of focusing on pre-conference meetings or staying focused on my objectives, I am totally freaking-out about resources.

This chapter is about mitigating these issues and providing several insights on what I pack when I travel.

First, and it seems like common sense, but I have travel packing lists. I use Microsoft Excel. One is for overnight trips. I also have packing lists for two-day, three-day, and a week of travel. These lists have the basics for clothing, business items, other accessories, and electronics.

I have traveled hundreds of times. When it comes to baggage, even though I travel a lot, I am not a fan of travelling with only carry-on bags. Yes, sometimes you save money. Yes, you save time not waiting for your checked bags. But unless your meeting is an hour after you land, which is normally bad planning, what is another 15 or 20 minutes?

I have travelled a hundred times with only carry-ons and another hundred with checked bags. This is very much a personal preference. For me, I find I have much more flexibility when I check a bag. But I still have a carry on for my computer and critical office files.

I can carry boxes of marketing collateral in a suitcase. No shipping to the hotel.

I can carry extension cords and a tripod for my video equipment in my suitcase.

The most important thing I carry? **My pillow.** I don't go anywhere without my pillow.

Anything I need to bring home, whether marketing collateral from the conference, a new customer binder, or a gift for my wife and kids, I always have room in a suitcase. I do not have to find a post office.

Everyone has a list. Well, you already know I travel with my pillow. A good night's sleep is critical to whatever meeting or event I'm attending.

Next to my pillow is my Bose noise cancellation headset. No knock-offs. Only Bose. Not the 'in the ear' version but the large over the ear headset. I do not use them for music. They are an absolute life-saver on the plane and in the hotel room when I am working. They cancel noise so well that I cannot hear the plane engines or my neighbors in the adjacent room. Yes, they are pricey at around $300 to $400. *But they are the absolute best travel investment I have ever made.*

Speaking of my Bose headset, they will also work with my phone so when I am taking a call in the airport, the hotel room, or especially at a trade show or conference, *I cannot hear anything but the person I am talking to.*

So, I have my pillow and my Bose headset. Next is my tablet with Kindle books. When I fly, I try not to work the entire time. The plane ride is my opportunity to recharge and relax before I go into full-business mode. There are a ton of folks who work on the plane. If that works for you, outstanding. I like to escape and read fiction and fantasy. I love books about magicians. All the business reading is done in the hotel room or back at the office.

No matter how much work you have, there is never enough time to relax and read your favorite novels. You have to find ways and times to recharge. That's me on a plane.

The next item is a Garmin car navigation system for the rental car. I do not travel anywhere in a rental car without one of these. You can buy one for less than a hundred dollars. Think about this - it costs an extra $8 a day for navigation when you rent a car. Buy your own Garmin and you will pay for it in less than five business trips. I have had my navigation system, an old Garmin, for more than five years. Had I rented a navigation system on every trip; I would have spent close to $500.

Three more key items. The first is a medicine bag. I travel with a small pharmacy. All the medicine I carry can fit into half the size of sandwich ziplock bag. A couple years ago I experienced two situations that required that I find a cab and spend an hour racing around the city to find a pharmacy or store open at two in the morning. Never again.

Yes, hotels sell aspirin and a few other items, but I had to pay $7 for two pills. I don't know about you, but paying that much for two aspirin is obnoxious. Whether it is Tylenol, antacids, Chapstick, or even pain pills, I have it.

I also carry a thumb drive. Actually, I carry three thumb drives and they all have the same data. Most of my thumb drives are 8GB drives. But my primary is a 256GB drive.

My office computer is a desktop. My travel computer is a laptop. I use Dropbox so I can access files from anywhere, but I always operate under Murphy's Law. I never assume I will be able to access the Internet. So, I carry all key files for my trip on thumb drives as a backup. Why three drives? If one of my drives fails, which eventually happens and always happens when you need it the most, I always have two backups.

Finally, I always travel with $200 in cash. I know, most people just carry their debit cards. But here is a story that will convince you that having cash is pretty darn important.

Imagine you were at a conference of more than 10,000 government contractors and you heard over the loud-speaker, "This is an emergency. We are immediately cancelling all events. Everyone needs to immediately initiate travel back home."

This happened to me. I was in Broward County Florida for the National DISA Conference. My rental car company called and said I had to immediately return my rental car. Instead of returning the car, I literally told them "not a chance." I told them I was changing my itinerary and dropping off the car at the first airport I could find to the North. They were not happy and I finally hung-up on them. Not the nicest thing I have done. They were only doing their job. But I had other priorities, such as saving my own life and getting out of dodge. I even invited two strangers to get in the car with me.

I drove two hours north, at a fairly high-rate of speed, to catch one of the last flights out of southern Florida.

That $200 was literally a life-saver. Phone lines were inundated and credit card authorizations were not going through. That cash enabled me to get gas and food. Huge cloud rings chased me as I drove eighty miles an hour.

I caught one of the last planes and barely got out of Florida before Hurricane Katrina hit. Unless you were there, you would not know that Katrina hit southern Florida before hammering New Orleans.

My key items are my pillow, the Bose noise cancellation headset, my kindle, a car navigation system, my travelling pharmacy, thumb drives for my critical data, and $200 cash.

Did I miss anything?

Something to think about.

Your Final Mission…
Should You Choose to Accept It

Thank you for reading my book! **PLEASE** leave a review on Amazon! Getting reviews is like pulling teeth!

Since its initial launch in January 2019, the book has been purchased by more than 10,000 companies, government contractors, and business professionals. The feedback has been inspiring!

If you enjoyed the book, perhaps laughed at my dry humor, and gained some value, I would be *very grateful* if you would do two things:

1. **Post a review on Amazon.** Even if you did not buy this book on Amazon, you can still leave a review! I hope you'll leave five stars!

2. **Take a picture of yourself holding this book and post the picture to LinkedIn** *and* say why you enjoyed the book. Please make sure to tag me – Joshua Frank in your post!

Publishing and marketing a book is not an easy task! My ability to share your picture with my network is 100 times more powerful than me saying, "Hey look, I have a good book."

Your support really does make a difference and I read all the reviews personally so I can get your feedback and improve this book.

Thanks again for your support!

Other Training Resources

Federal Access (FA)
Knowledge-Base and Training Platform

The flagship solution of RSM Federal. Federal Access (FA) is an award winning and nationally-recognized training platform that helps companies win government contracts. Federal Access is not a bid-matching tool. Federal Access provides award-winning templates and business strategies that you need to win government contracts. Learn more at
https://rsmfederal.com/FA

Connect with Joshua Frank on LinkedIn

If you gained value from the content and concepts in this book, the author often provides similar value via articles and posts on LinkedIn.
https://www.linkedin.com/in/joshuapfrank/

Podcast
Game Changers for Government Contractors

Available on iTunes and Soundcloud, Game Changers is the most listened-to podcast in the nation for small business government contractors. Every month, two or more industry subject matter experts provide game-changing strategies for winning government contracts.
https://rsmfederal.com/gamechangers

The Government Sales Manual

This manual is a definitive guide on selling to the government. If you enjoyed this book, you will truly enjoy *The Government Sales Manual*. Whether you are new to the government market or been selling for 10 years, it is one of the most comprehensive resources on the market. 460 pages with hundreds of techniques and strategies. To learn more about The Government Sales Manual, available at rsmfederal.com and on Amazon.
(Check both sites as I often run discounts on one or the other.)

About the Author

JOSHUA FRANK is managing partner for RSM Federal. Bestselling author, trainer, and management consultant with 30 years in the government market, Josh is a recognized authority on government sales and speaks nationally on small business strategy and business acceleration. He lives in St. Louis, Missouri with his wife, son, and daughter. Josh loves helping business owners accelerate their government sales.

Josh specializes in the development and implementation of techniques and strategies required to differentiate, position for, and win government contracts. His marketing strategies, highly educational and thought-provoking, are consistently rated as one of the strongest sessions at national conferences and events.

Due to the number of contracts won by Josh's clients, he was awarded Veteran Business Owner of the Year by the Small Business Administration (SBA) (a first for a business coach) and the National Industry Small Business Advocate of the Year by the Society of American Military Engineers (SAME). Josh's company was also awarded "The 50 Most Trustworthy Companies of the Year" by Silicon Review.

An avid outdoor enthusiast, Girl Scout and Boy Scout leader, Josh lives in St. Louis, Missouri with his wife, daughter, and son. He is a former military intelligence officer with an undergraduate degree in English, a Masters in Management Information Systems (MIS), and a Master's in Business Administration (MBA).

Author's Website
authorjoshfrank.com

Learn more about RSM Federal
rsmfederal.com

Accelerate Your Sales
Federal Access Knowledge-Base
rsmfederal.com/federal-access

FREE podcasts for government contractors at
https://soundcloud.com/gamechangersforgovernmentcontractors